JEEP TRANSFER CASES

HOW TO REBUILD

Trenton McGee

CarTech®

CarTech®

CarTech®, Inc.
6118 Main Street
North Branch, MN 55056
Phone: 651-277-1200 or 800-551-4754
Fax: 651-277-1203
www.cartechbooks.com

Edit by Wes Eisenschenk
Layout by Connie DeFlorin

ISBN 978-1-61325-773-9
Item No. SA538

Library of Congress Cataloging-in-Publication Data Available

Written, edited, and designed in the U.S.A.
Printed in China
10 9 8 7 6 5 4 3 2 1

All photos are courtesy of author Trenton McGee unless otherwise noted.

Back Cover: The photo of the author is courtesy of Rachel Speir.

DISTRIBUTION BY:

Europe
PGUK
63 Hatton Garden
London EC1N 8LE, England
Phone: 020 7061 1980 • Fax: 020 7242 3725
www.pguk.co.uk

Australia
Renniks Publications Ltd.
3/37-39 Green Street
Banksmeadow, NSW 2109, Australia
Phone: 2 9695 7055 • Fax: 2 9695 7355
www.renniks.com

Canada
Login Canada
300 Saulteaux Crescent
Winnipeg, MB, R3J 3T2 Canada
Phone: 800 665 1148 • Fax: 800 665 0103
www.lb.ca

TABLE OF CONTENTS

Rebuild Procedure Directions

In many instances during the rebuild process, I provided the direction (front or rear, upward or downward, and inward or outward). Since the direction is dependent on the orientation of the object in relation to the reader, this can be confusing. So, I always use the terms “front” or “rear” as well as “upward” or “downward” assuming that the transfer case is positioned as it is when it is installed on the vehicle (with the front output shaft being on the front of the case and the rear output shaft being on the back of the case). The terms “inward” and “outward” are noted from the center of the transfer case.

CHAPTER 1

Transfer Case History and Identification

Before diving into the nuts and bolts of rebuilding the most common and popular transfer cases that Jeep has used through more than 80 years (and counting) of production, it's helpful to understand some of the history and variations of the various transfer cases.

In this chapter, I cover the particulars of the transfer cases that this book shows how to rebuild as well as how to identify some of the other transfer cases that Jeep has used over the years. Although these other transfer cases are not the subject of a detailed rebuild procedure here, it is helpful to be able to identify them, know what models they were used on, and know some of their attributes and drawbacks.

This is my 1997 Jeep Wrangler–based, rock-crawling buggy on the trails in Moab, Utah. Transfer cases are a critical part of any 4x4. They make the traction of four-wheel drive possible, which enables backcountry exploration.

Dana 18

The Dana 18 transfer case is one of the components that made the Jeep a legendary vehicle in World War II and later during

The Dana 18 is the only cast-iron Jeep transfer case with the front and rear output yokes offset to the passenger's side. It is a cast-iron, gear-driven case. In addition, a Dana 18 can be identified by a thin stamped-steel inspection cover on the back of the case that is in line with the input gear. Although, an overdrive or power take-off (PTO) gearbox could be in the place of this cover. Many Dana 18s also had a parking-brake assembly mounted on the rear output flange (as seen here).

civilian production. Two aspects that led to the Jeep's quick ascent to iconic status were its toughness and the superior traction of four-wheel drive (4WD). 4WD doesn't work without a gearbox that splits engine torque between the front and rear axles and that gearbox needs to be extraordinarily tough to be reliable. The Dana 18 is both tough and reliable.

As one of the first mass-produced transfer cases ever made, the design was so good that it was used for nearly 30 years in a variety of different Jeep vehicles. The Dana 18 was also used in a variety of International trucks, most notably the Scout 80 and, later, the Scout 800. Although a few improvements and refinements were made throughout its production run, the Dana 18 remained largely unchanged, and the genius of its basic design can be seen in some other legendary transfer cases that came later (the Dana 20 and Dana 300).

The Dana 18 is the only mass-produced Jeep transfer case that has a cast-iron case with both the front and rear outputs offset to the passenger's side of the vehicle, which is known as "passenger-side drop." Early Bantams and Ford GPs used front and rear axles with differentials that were offset to the driver's side, which necessitated driver-side-drop Dana 18s. However, in the interest of standardization and parts interchangeability between the Ford GPW and the Willys MB, the axles were switched to passenger-side drop, and the Dana 18 was changed to passenger-side drop at the same time.

So, while it is possible to find driver-side-drop Dana 18s, they are exceedingly rare and best saved for an early Bantam or Ford GP restoration project. One notable advantage to the dual-offset design is that both differentials (the lowest hanging portion of the vehicle) are in line with one another, as opposed to later Jeeps that have a centered rear differential and an offset front differential. A savvy driver can use the dual-offset design as an advantage over rough terrain, knowing that the lowest portion of the vehicle is to the right of center and thus pick a driving line that avoids obstacles.

Identification and Features

The most notable features for Dana 18 identification are its cast-iron case and passenger-side drop. The center-rear portion of the Dana 18 has a thin metal power take-off (PTO) cover that is retained by five bolts in stock form, but there could be an auxiliary overdrive housing or even a PTO gearbox in place of this cover, which is mentioned in Chapter 2.

The rear output often incorporates a drum parking brake, but this brake assembly can be (and often is) removed without impacting the operation of the transfer case. The transmission bolt pattern of the transfer case is shaped roughly like the state of Texas but backward, and it attaches to the back of the transmission with five 3/8-inch mounting bolts. On the bottom of

All Jeep and International Dana 18s used the five-bolt "backward Texas" bolt pattern to mate to the back of the transmission.

Most Dana 18s (or, as this tag indicates, technically Spicer 18s) had a tag that was riveted to the top of the case. However, these tags are often missing or have become unreadable. This tag is only visible if the transfer case has been removed from the vehicle.

the transfer case is a stamped-steel inspection cover (aftermarket covers are often made of aluminum) that is retained by 10 bolts.

The front output shaft is a 10-spline unit and accepts a Spicer 1310 U-joint in stock form. The rear output is also a 10-spline unit in stock form but is a flange style to accommodate the parking brake, rather than a traditional yoke. However, the rear can easily be converted to a traditional yoke if needed.

The Dana 18 has two modes of operation (two-wheel drive [2WD] and 4WD) as well as two ranges (high and low).

Most civilian Dana 18s have a 2.46:1 low-range ratio, but there was also a very rare 2.43:1 variation. All military Dana 18s had a 1.97:1 ratio. All Dana 18s that were used in military vehicles and even the civilian CJs have a twin-stick transfer case, which means that there are two sticks on the floor to operate the ranges of the case. The left stick controls 2WD and 4WD, while the right controls high and low range. There are also single-stick Dana 18s (mostly in V-6-powered trucks and SUVs), where a single lever controls both of the modes and ranges.

Applications and Variations

The Dana 18 was used in the following vehicles:

- Bantam Reconnaissance Car (BRC) (prototype military development vehicles)
- Willys MA and MB
- Ford GP, GPW, and Pygmy
- Kaiser and Kaiser Willys CJ-2, CJ-2A, CJ-3A, CJ-3B, M38, M38A1, CJ-5, CJ-6, FC-150 and 170 (and military variants), utility trucks and wagons through 1971
- International Scout 80 and 800

Novak Conversions, which is one of the leading authorities on Jeep drivetrains and an excellent source for technical knowledge and rebuild parts, provides a breakdown of the Dana 18 and its variations. The company divided the Dana 18 into five major styles based on the production years of the vehicles that utilized the Dana 18. This breakdown comes with some major caveats, and it's never a good idea to make assumptions about the parts that are installed on a Jeep based only on the year of the body or even what's on the title.

Dana 18 Applications

Several versions of the Dana 18 transfer case were used from 1941 to 1971.

Early Military: 1941–1945

All military versions of the Dana 18 were married to the T-84 3-speed transmission and have a 3/4-inch-diameter intermediate shaft. These also feature a 1.97:1 low-range ratio and dual shifters as well as a $3^{5}/_{32}$-inch input locating bore.

Due to age, these are not as prevalent today and are generally not as desirable as the later versions mostly because of the small intermediate shaft and the higher low-range ratio. The small intermediate shaft is more of a longevity concern than a strength concern when it is used at the higher speeds (and higher internal-gear RPM) of modern traffic.

Early Civilian: 1945–1946

Some oddball variants of the early civilian CJs were produced, including a side-shift or column-shift version of the T-90 that was mated to a Dana 18 with a 3/4-inch-diameter intermediate shaft and a 2.43:1 low range. These are exceedingly rare but are worth mentioning. According to Novak Conversions, these obscure variants were used in the preproduction CJ-1, the 1944 to 1945 CJ-2, and the CJ-2A through serial number 24196.

Of course, due to age and the wide interchangeability of parts, these oddball components could show up anywhere in the early CJ line, although the column shift would be difficult and cumbersome to install in a Jeep that wasn't originally equipped with one.

Mid Civilian: 1946–1955

Even as World War II was still winding down, Willys recognized that the utility of the Jeep extended well beyond military use, and it made several improvements to the Jeep to expand its versatility and appeal to civilian users.

A lower low-range ratio of 2.46:1 that remained throughout the subsequent production of the Dana 18 was among the items that were changed. The diameter of the intermediate shaft was increased to $1^{1}/_{8}$ inches with caged needle-roller bearings. This was the era when many companies began making use of the PTO port, manufacturing a variety of different accessories that were used to drive a wide range of pumps, plows, implements, winches, post-hole diggers, and more. This era covers all of the traditional flat-fender models (CJ-2A, CJ-3A, M38, and CJ-3B).

Later Civilian: 1955–1966

About the time that Jeep fenders started getting round with the introduction of the CJ-5 in 1955, the Dana 18 was improved again, as the intermediate shaft was increased to

The only major variation of the Dana 18 was the use of three different-diameter intermediate shafts (arrow) throughout its production run: 3/4 inch, $1^{1}/_{8}$ inch, and 1¼ inch. Measure the diameter of the intermediate shaft of your case before ordering a rebuild kit, even if you know the year of the Jeep that the transfer case came from.

Dana 18 Applications *continued*

1¼ inches in diameter. This change varies a little, depending on the Jeep model.

According to Novak Conversions, this was done not so much to improve strength but to increase the bearing surface area and the number of bearings due to the faster road speeds that were possible with more powerful engines. This change also marked the return of uncaged roller bearings for the intermediate shaft, which allowed more rollers but also increased difficulty when it came time to rebuild the case. Transmissions other than the T-90 began to be coupled to the Dana 18 during this era.

Final Civilian: 1966–1971

The final large-case version of the Dana 18 was arguably the best. It was found exclusively behind Buick V-6 engines and was mated to the T-86 or T-14 transmission.

This larger case was the sign of things to come, as it is actually the same housing as the Dana 20, which replaced the Dana 18. Until this point, the Dana 18 had used a 3 5/32-inch-diameter input bore, but the bore was increased to 4 inches with this version. This case also lost the provision for the shifter mounting point on the transfer case, as the single lever was mounted to the transmission via a bracket.

Although it uses a Dana 20 case, the internals of this version are mostly identical to a standard Dana 18, which essentially makes it a Dana 20 with the guts of a Dana 18. It's possible to make a "Super 18" by combining a Dana 18 and a Dana 20 and copying this variation's arrangement.

Although build records are reasonably accurate, Jeeps were manufactured by smaller companies than the Big Three manufacturers (Ford, General Motors, and Chrysler). As a result, year splits for minor changes are inexact. If parts from a previous model were left over and those parts worked on a newer model, the old parts were installed until they ran out. Then, the new parts would be installed.

To further muddy the waters, most military and civilian Jeep parts interchange from 1941 to about 1954, and with about 80 years between when these rolled off the assembly line and today, there's no telling what someone might have changed at some point in a Jeep's life. Indeed, it's rare to see a flat-fender Jeep that's 100-percent original. It's common to see Jeeps that have been pieced together from three or more different models, which indicates a long lineage of desirability among military, industrial, and recreational users.

Strength and Swapability

Thanks in part to its simple design and compact nature, the Dana 18 is highly desirable in short-wheelbase applications, such as early flat-fender Jeeps, where there's simply not a lot of room for something longer. It has proven to withstand V-8 power, compound gearing, and heavy use while remaining just as reliable as it was with stock flatheads and small tires.

However, the Dana 18 is not immune to failure when subjected to excessive abuse. The helical design of the gears places outward pressure on the case, and case cracks are somewhat common between the inspection-cover hole and the PTO port. The front output-shaft gear is fairly small in diameter and can fail either at the gear itself or the inner support bushing. The offset design of the case, with the front and rear outputs offset to the passenger's side of the case, tends to make drivetrain wrap or twist a concern with non-stock engines. This offset design precludes the Dana 18 from being used in modern applications with a centered rear axle, but there are other good transfer cases that eliminate the need to use the Dana 18 in non-offset applications.

Another telltale sign of the Dana 18 is the mounting foot cast into the front output-shaft housing. This mounting foot helps combat the stresses and rotation of having both output shafts offset in relation to the centerline of the rest of the drivetrain.

Overdrives and PTOs

Several components have been manufactured over the years to enhance the utility of the Dana 18 and the Jeep as a whole. The most famous and well known of these is the Warn overdrive. Sold in the 1960s and early 1970s as an add-on to the Dana 18, this unit added a 0.78 overdrive gear to the stock 3-speed transmission.

A very well-designed unit, the lever-operated overdrive can be used in any gear to "split" gears—even reverse. This was an extremely popular addition at the time, and these units are highly sought after, even today. Although Warn was the largest manufacturer of overdrives for the Dana 18, Husky, Dual-Matic, and BorgWarner offered similar products. Warn eventually sold the tooling for the overdrive to Advance Adapters, which made several revisions and marketed it as the Saturn overdrive, and it still does so to this day. Another company, Herm the Overdrive Guy, offers a wide range of parts and rebuild services for the original Warn units and even has a limited amount of support for the other overdrive brands.

In addition to overdrives, several PTO boxes were manufactured to power a wide range of implements. I've seen PTO units for front-mounted accessories, rear-mounted accessories, and sometimes both. Also, belt- and gear-driven units have been created to power bed-mounted accessories, such as pumps, generators, compressors, etc. Several implements were manufactured that were powered by these PTOs, including plows, rakes, three-point hitches, mowers, winches, post-hole diggers, wrecker booms, and much more. Although parts can be hard to find for many of these PTO gearboxes, a little ingenuity and mechanical know-how can bring most of them back into service with enough patience, time, and effort.

A Warn overdrive is a common and popular upgrade that can be added to any Dana 18 transfer case. This cylindrical-shaped auxiliary gearbox that is mounted in place of the inspection cover offers a 25-percent or 30-percent overdrive, depending on when the unit was manufactured. These, as well as a wide range of PTO gearboxes, are highly sought-after accessories that can greatly enhance the driveability and versatility of an older Jeep.

The biggest threats to the Dana 18's reliability today are age and inferior overseas replacement parts.

With the newest Dana 18 being more than 50 years old, mileage and the elements take their toll. In nearly all cases, the Dana 18 shares gear oil with the transmission, and it's extremely common to find internal water damage due to water leaking past the transmission-shifter cane on an open-top vehicle. Water contamination wreaks havoc on gear faces and causes heavy pitting. It also ruins bearings and other parts. While replacement gears are readily available, not all of them are close to being as good as the originals.

Several overseas companies reproduce these components. Some have more success and attention to quality control than others.

The intermediate shafts are problematic, as a large number of people have reported poor hardening of the intermediate shaft in many of the less-expensive rebuild kits that are available. When sourcing replacement gears, try and find serviceable used or new old stock (NOS) parts when possible. As for rebuild kits, ask questions and check the reviews before purchasing.

Novak Conversions is one of the only companies I know of that has its intermediate shafts built to its specifications, with hardening that meets or exceeds OEM specifications. Aside from using highly specialized equipment, there is no way to check a gear or shaft's hardness with a visual inspection, which makes it difficult for the layman to differentiate a good part from a bad one.

Due to its reputation for strength and an extremely long production run, Dana 18 parts remain plentiful and easy to obtain. Rebuild kits are readily available from several sources (with caveats), as are adapters that enable the Dana 18 to be used behind a wide range of both classic and modern transmissions. When shopping for a Dana 18, look for one with the larger 1¼-inch intermediate shaft because that's the version that is most likely capable of holding up at modern freeway speeds. When it's properly maintained, there's no reason why a Dana 18 couldn't provide another 80 years of reliable service under any Jeep vehicle.

Dana 20

As with the Dana 18, the Dana 20 enjoyed a long production run and was used by a wide variety of OEMs. In fact, the Dana 20 is essentially a redesign of the venerable Dana 18 and even shares some internal parts with its predecessor.

Applications and Variations

First introduced in 1962 in Jeep vehicles, the Dana 20 was used in a variety of Jeep models (from CJs to full-size trucks and Wagoneers) through 1979.

In addition, the Dana 20 was used by other OEMs, including International, Ford, and Chevrolet for a limited time. Jeep and International Dana 20s are quite similar and share many internal parts as well as the "backward Texas" input bolt pattern that the Dana 18 used.

The six-spline input gear in manual applications is another carryover from the Dana 18. In many cases, this means that a Dana 20 can be installed behind a transmission that originally mated to a Dana 18 (and vice versa). However, some automatic versions of the Dana 20 used different input spline counts, which can complicate interchangeability. Ford Dana 20s share some internal components with the Jeep and International versions but look different and have a different transmission bolt pattern. Another Dana 20 variation was used by Chevrolet from 1966 to 1973, but these are exceedingly rare and have almost nothing in common with the versions that were used by the other manufacturers.

The Jeep Dana 20 has dual modes (2WD and 4WD), dual ranges (high and low), and a neutral position. It has a 1:1 direct drive in high range and a 2:1

The Dana 20 resembles the Dana 18, which came before it, and the Dana 300, which came after it. Like the others, it is a cast-iron, gear-driven transfer case. The biggest telltale sign of a Dana 20 is the centered rear output (unlike a Dana 18) as well as a cast-iron rear output housing (as opposed to the Dana 300's aluminum rear output). The shape of the Dana 20's rear output as well as the bearing cover on the back of the front output are also slightly different from a Dana 300, but you have to compare them side by side to see the differences.

The Dana 20 shares the "backward Texas" five-bolt mounting pattern with the Dana 18, and because of this, the Dana 20 and Dana 18 are largely interchangeable. Another clue that identifies a Dana 20 is having no shifter mounting provisions in the shifter housing as well as the "wing" on the front output housing that hangs off slightly past the passenger-side edge of the main case. All Jeep Dana 20s had a front output offset to the passenger's side. Bronco Dana 20s were offset to the driver's side.

low range. It features a cast-iron case and is entirely gear driven, which means that no chains are used to transfer power. It is extremely compact (only 10½ inches long) and has a proven reputation for being extremely strong for its size. The Dana 20 was used behind everything from anemic 4-cylinder engines to healthy V-8s, and it performs well in a number of heavy-duty applications.

The stock 2:1 low range is somewhat disappointing for rock-crawling enthusiasts, but some options are available to improve it. It's possible to retrofit the 2.46:1 low range from a Bronco Dana 20 into a Jeep version, and an aftermarket low-range kit of 3.15:1 is available through Teraflex and Advance Adapters. These upgrades aren't covered in the scope of this book, but the installation steps for both are quite similar to the traditional rebuild, which is detailed in Chapter 3.

Model 21

A Model 21 transfer case was used by Jeep and Ford for a short time. This transfer case was a single-speed version of the Dana 20 with no low range. Some early- to mid-1960s full-size Wagoneers and Gladiators used them, but they were somewhat unusual even then and are fairly rare today.

Identifying Features

Identifying a Dana 20 is relatively simple due to visual cues that set it apart from the Dana 18 and Dana 300, which both look similar. The easiest way to differentiate a Dana 20 from a Dana 18 is the centered rear output that is in line with the input. (Dana 18s had an offset rear output.) A Dana 20 has a cast-iron rear output housing that is shaped slightly differently than the aluminum rear output of the Dana 300. In addition, the Dana 20 has the backward-Texas transmission bolt pattern that differs from the six-bolt round pattern of the Dana 300.

The Jeep Dana 20 stayed consistent mechanically throughout its production run. The only significant difference was that early Dana 20s used 10-spline output yokes, while later ones used 26-spline yokes. There were several different shifter arrangements used among the wide range of Jeep models, some of which can be quite odd and problematic. As a result, it's best to retain the shift mechanism for the vehicle when swapping a Dana 20 or to source one from a similar model to what you're working on. A twin-stick shifter is a popular and worthwhile upgrade for off-road enthusiasts because it offers the ability to have two-wheel low range or front-wheel-drive high range if the interlock pill is removed from the shift-rail assembly.

Strength and Swapability

The Dana 20 is an extremely strong and compact transfer case, which makes it desirable to retain in any stock application. It is also a decent swap candidate for a custom build. Due to the popularity of the Dana 20 and its shared bolt pattern with the Dana 18, a variety of non-stock manual and automatic transmissions can be mated to the Dana 20 thanks to aftermarket support from companies such as Advance Adapters and Novak Conversions.

As with many older transfer cases, the biggest enemies to the Dana 20 are age and the elements. Water contamination is common due to its shared oiling with the transmission, so inspect the internals of a Dana 20 closely before purchasing. Rebuild kits and some internal parts are common, but other internal components can be difficult to locate.

Dana 300

The Dana 300 had a comparatively short lifespan compared to other Jeep transfer cases. However, what it lacked in its production run, it more than made up with sheer brute strength.

Identifying Features

The Dana 300 and Dana 20 can be difficult to differentiate with a casual glance, mainly because the Dana 300 was a further refinement of the Dana 20. The biggest telltale signs to identify a Dana 300 are the asymmetrical 6-bolt round input bolt pattern and a fixed 23-spline internal input shaft. The Dana 300 also differs from the Dana 20 in that the front and rear output shaft housings are aluminum rather than cast iron.

In addition, the Dana 300 has built-in provisions for the shifter in the front output housing that the Dana 20 does not have. The rear bearing cap for the Dana 300's front output shaft is also a slightly different

From the rear, a Dana 300 looks very similar to a Dana 20, especially when the rear output housing is painted black (as is the case here). However, sticking a magnet on the rear output housing of a Dana 300 reveals a housing made of aluminum (as opposed to cast iron). The rear cap for the front output shaft is also shaped slightly differently.

The smoking gun to identify a Dana 300 is to examine the input bolt pattern, which is an asymmetrical, six-bolt, round pattern with an aluminum plate around the input gear. There's also the aluminum front output housing that has ears cast into it to mount the transfer-case shifters.

shape than the Dana 20's rear bearing cap. Even with these differences, you can study photos of both transfer cases to pick up these and other visual cues that differentiate them.

As one of the best transfer cases ever made, you'd be hard-pressed to find a mass-produced OEM transfer case that offers the strength, small footprint, and relative light weight of the Dana 300. Because of these and other attributes, the Dana 300 remains a very popular choice to swap into a variety of Jeep models and even non-Jeep applications. It was such a good design that it was largely copied and then improved upon considerably with the Atlas transfer case, which is manufactured with Advance Adapters and is the gold standard for a transfer case among recreational off-roaders and racers.

The Dana 300 is a cast-iron, gear-driven transfer case that has a 2.62:1 low range. Although 2.62:1 is a relatively tall low-range gear by modern standards, it was a big improvement over the Dana 20, which offered only a 2.03:1 low-range ratio. While the difference doesn't seem very big on paper, it's important to remember that gearing is multiplicative.

For example, take a Jeep with a T-18 wide-ratio transmission that has a 6.32:1 first gear and 3.73 axle gears. With a Dana 20, calculating the final-drive ratio looks like this: 6.32 x 2.03 x 3.73 = 47.85. With a Dana 300, it looks like this: 6.32 x 2.62 x 3.73 = 61.76. That simple change in transfer-case ratio drops the final drive from about 48:1 to 62:1. That's a big difference in torque multiplication and slow-speed control over difficult terrain.

Applications and Variations

The Dana 300 has three variations. Two are specific to Jeeps and one is specific to Internationals. The most common variation was used from 1980–1986 in CJ-7s and can be identified by a six-bolt, round input pattern (where it mates to the back of the transmission) and an internal 23-spline input gear.

The oddball Jeep Dana 300 was used in 1980 and in CJ-5s only, which features the same input pattern and spline count but uses a shorter rear output shaft than the later models. Although the shorter output shaft can be considered advantageous, it's really not because parts are scarce for these one-year-only cases, and they can't be converted to the later style.

The International Scout Dana 300 was produced in 1980 only and is easily identified by the Texas-style bolt pattern that is shared with the Jeep/International Dana 18 and Dana 20. Although it's desirable on paper as a direct replacement for a Dana 18 or Dana 20, it's not very sought after because it's quite rare, parts availability is scarce, and it shares little in common with its Jeep equivalents.

Because of the extreme popularity of the Dana 300, several aftermarket upgrades are available. The rear output shaft is known to shear at the spiral-cut speedometer drive gears under extreme use, but heavy-duty, 32-spline output shafts are available from Advance Adapters and JB Conversions. A similar heavy-duty front output-shaft upgrade is available from JB Conversions. Further, the 2.64:1 low range can be greatly improved with a 4:1 LoMax gear conversion, which is also available from JB Conversions. Adding the gearing and output upgrades to a standard Dana 300 brings the strength and capability of a Dana 300 into Atlas territory, and the cost may also be comparable, depending on what other parts that your stock Dana 300 might need.

Strength and Swapability

Lending to the popularity of the Dana 300 and its use of a 6-bolt, round, 23-spline input pattern that became the standard for Jeep transfer cases for decades following the Dana 300's introduction, the sky is the limit regarding which transmissions can be successfully adapted to it.

Thanks to aftermarket support from companies such as Novak Conversions, Advance Adapters, and JB Conversions, just about any popular manual or automatic transmission can be mated to the Dana 300. Of particular note is a clocking ring, which enables the transfer case to be clocked upward at a variety of angles to improve ground clearance. In addition, the clocking ring can change the driveline angle.

Dana 300 flip kits are also available, allowing the 300 to be run upside down for a driver-side-drop application. However, these are known to leak past the shift rail seals and have oiling problems.

If it sounds like the Dana 300 is *the* passenger-drop transfer case to have, it is because of its strength and adapting options.

NP231

The New Process 231 (NP231) transfer case featured several major changes in Jeep transfer-case design.

First, it has an aluminum case, while all of the previous Jeep transfer cases were primarily cast iron. Second, the NP231 is chain driven, which means that the front output shaft is driven by a large chain inside the transfer case, rather than gear driven like all of the others. Last but not least, the NP231 transfer cases have the front output shaft offset to the driver's side rather than the passenger's side, which makes them incompatible with older Jeeps that were all passenger-side drop.

One of the reasons for these changes is weight; a chain is relatively lightweight compared to using a series of gears to transfer power. Another reason is quiet operation and reduced friction; chains are relatively quiet and introduce less drag than a series of interlocking gears. A third reason is ease of manufacturing; a chain is cheaper and easier to produce than a series of helical-cut gears.

When the NP231 was first introduced, some feared that chain-driven cases in general were weaker than gear-driven cases. However, that proved to be false. The NP231 and several transfer cases of similar design have performed well with V-8 power, low gearing, big tires, and heavy abuse. In fact, almost all modern transfer cases that are in use today, including those for 1-ton diesels that make close to 1,000 ft-lbs of torque from the factory, use a chain-driven case with an aluminum housing. Even the lighter-duty transfer cases, such as the NP231, can be made significantly stronger with some internal upgrades, much of which is detailed in Chapter 5.

It's easy to differentiate a New Process transfer case from most earlier Jeep transfer cases. The dead giveaways are the oval-shaped, aluminum case; bolts around the perimeter that hold the case halves together; and the red and silver tag that is riveted to the center of the rear case half. Differentiating New Process transfer cases from one another at a casual glance is a different story, as most of them look quite similar.

The one strength caveat of the aluminum case is impact resistance. It doesn't take much of a rock impact to break an aluminum case, while a cast-iron case can take a much harder hit. Therefore, adequately protecting an NP231 with skid plates is very important on a dedicated off-roading vehicle.

Applications and Variations

The NP231 transfer case had a long production run in Jeeps. It first appeared in 1988 in YJ Wranglers, XJ Cherokees, and MJ Comanches. It was used during the full run of YJs and most of the MJs starting in 1988, while the Cherokee had a few different transfer cases available aside from the NP231 (depending on the year and options package). A telltale sign of a non-NP231 XJ is if it has a full-time 4WD range selection. In that case, the vehicle is equipped with an NP242 transfer case.

NP231s continued to be used in the TJ Wrangler throughout most of its production run until being replaced in 2005. NP231s can be found behind automatic and manual transmissions, and internal parts largely interchange with a few notable exceptions that are detailed during the rebuild section in Chapter 5. All NP231s in Jeeps behind a 4-cylinder engine had a 21-spline input shaft, while all NP231s in 6-cylinder engines had a 23-spline input. The input shafts can be swapped fairly easily, but the procedure requires a complete disassembly of the case.

Jeep NP231 transfer cases used either a 21- or 23-spline input shaft and an asymmetrical, 6-bolt, round bolt pattern. Dodge cases were also usually 23-spline. Chevy cases used a 5-bolt pattern and a different spline count.

Identifying Features

The easiest way to identify an NP231 (and differentiate it from other transfer cases that look similar) is to look at the circular tag that is riveted to the center of the back of the case. Jeep NP231 transfer cases are stamped with "NP231J."

Chevy and Dodge versions of the NP231 were also produced. On the identification tag, Chevy cases are stamped with "NP231C," and Dodge cases are stamped with "NP231D." The Chevy versions have a five-bolt pattern that is incompatible with the six-bolt pattern of the Dodge and Jeep transfer cases. Input-shaft spline counts and lengths vary among these cases, but many internal parts interchange. Even so, as plentiful as these transfer cases are, it's best to just stick with a Jeep transfer case, rather than attempting to mix and match parts.

In addition, NP231HD transfer cases were used in ZJ Grand Cherokees, Dodge trucks, and some Chevy trucks with a six-pinion planetary gearset and a wider chain that's a significant strength upgrade over the three-pinion planetary in the lighter NP231s. How to swap in these larger components is covered in Chapter 5, and it's a worthy upgrade for any NP231 that will see some abuse. Lastly, there's a very worthwhile tailshaft upgrade that replaces the failure-prone slip-yoke-style tailshaft to a much-stronger fixed yoke. A slip-yoke-eliminator (SYE) kit shortens the overall length of the transfer case at the same time and is another upgrade that is covered in Chapter 5.

The most accurate way to identify an NP231 or any other New Process transfer case is to examine the circular red and silver tag. The model number is listed at the top, and it's usually followed by a letter. In this case, the "J" after "231" indicates that this is a Jeep transfer case. A "D" would indicate a case from a Dodge truck, and a "C" would indicate a case from a Chevy truck.

Strength and Swapability

The NP231 is a strong and durable transfer case, especially when upgraded with an SYE kit. As mentioned earlier, the NP231 is a driver-side-drop transfer case, so it is incompatible with any of the earlier Jeep passenger-side-offset axles. It shares a six-bolt, round bolt pattern with the Dana 300, and this same pattern was used for many subsequent years. Those in 4-cylinder applications had a 21-spline input gear, while the 6-cylinder versions had a 23-spline input gear. Input gears are easy to change but require transfer case disassembly.

Because the input gears and bolt patterns were standardized by the time that the NP231 was put into production, it's pretty easy to swap an NP231 into a number of contemporary Jeeps with automatic or manual transmissions. Several adapters are available to make just about any non-stock transmission work. This is due to the Atlas transfer case utilizing the same 6-bolt pattern and 23-spline input. There were also some variations in stock input-gear length, so pay attention to spline length and engagement when working with a non-stock application.

NP207, NP208, NP219, NP228, and NP229

Starting in 1980, major changes took place in various full-size Jeep models, migrating from a traditional passenger-side-drop front axle to a driver-side drop. This shift also saw the introduction and subsequent widespread use of chain-driven transfer cases with aluminum housings, as opposed to gear-driven, cast-iron transfer cases. All of the transfer cases in this family offered a 2.61:1 low range.

Applications and Variations

The NP207 and NP208 were the first of these transfer cases, offering the ordinary ranges of 2-Hi as well as locked 4-Hi and 4-Low. These were used in J-series trucks from 1980–1987 and full-size Cherokees from 1980–1983. There were GM and Ford versions of the NP208 in the same era, but they had different cases, bolt patterns, and input-spline counts than the Jeep versions.

The NP219 was a full-time 4WD variant that was produced by New Process. It offered a glimpse into the future, offering a viscous coupling that biased torque between the front and rear axles in high range. It was only used in full-size Jeeps for two years when it was replaced by the NP228 and NP229. The NP228 differed from the NP219 in that it had an open differential for full-time operation (rather than a viscous coupling), but it also offered a locked 4-Hi mode as well as 4-Low. The NP228 was also vacuum actuated (rather than using traditional levers for engaging the various ranges), and this vacuum system often was problematic. The NP229 was quite similar to the NP228 but marked the return of a viscous coupling for torque biasing in high range rather than an open differential. The NP229 was used in full-size Grand Wagoneers until the end of the production run in 1991.

The NP207 appeared in 1984 with the first midsize Cherokee XJs as well as the first year of production (1987) for the YJ Wrangler. Very similar to the NP231 that replaced it, the NP207's primary difference was a wider chain and the use of spur-cut planetary gears (as opposed to helical-cut gears), which made them noisier in low range. As with the NP231, The NP207 used an asymmetrical 6-bolt pattern and either a 21- or 23-spline input. Although it's not technically a bad transfer case, its easy interchangeability with the more-popular and better-supported NP231 makes it a less-desirable case for anyone building a serious off-roader.

Identifying Features

These early New Process transfer cases often have a circular tag on the back that has the model number of the case, but sometimes they do not. They all

Jeep NP208s were made in both driver-side and passenger-side configurations to accommodate the switch from passenger-side offset front differentials to driver-side differentials in 1980. This particular NP208 is a passenger-side-drop version with a slip yoke, but I have seen versions of this case with fixed yokes in both configurations.

have a ribbed aluminum housing with bolts around the perimeter that hold the two case halves together.

Strength and Swapability

With the exception of the NP207, this family of transfer cases should be largely interchangeable among one another, at least in terms of the bolt pattern. Some of these were not used for very long and not much is known about them, but considering that a few models only were used for a couple of years indicates that they were problematic. Of this family, the NP208 is the most desirable because of its largely trouble-free operation and traditional part-time four-wheel drive. As previously stated, the NP207 used in early XJs and YJs isn't a bad transfer case, but its interchangeability with the better-supported NP231 makes it less desirable by default.

The NP242 looks strikingly similar to the NP231, and they are difficult to differentiate without looking at the identification tag. This particular NP242 is equipped with an SYE kit from Tom Woods Driveshafts. (Photo Courtesy Verne Simons)

NP242

The successor to the NP229, the NP242 is one of the better-regarded, full-time-capable transfer cases that Jeep used.

Marketed as the SelectTrac option on XJ Cherokees and MJ Comanches, these transfer cases offered 2-Hi, 4-Hi with torque biasing (48/52 front/rear), 4-Hi Lock (50/50 torque split to both axles), Neutral, and 4-Low (also locked).

Applications and Variations

As an option beginning in 1987, the NP242 was offered beside the NP231 for the remainder of the XJ Cherokee's production run through 2001 and continued briefly with the KJ Liberty in 2002. It was also used throughout the production run of the ZJ Grand Cherokee from 1993 to 1998 and the WJ Grand Cherokee from 1999 to 2004. GM versions of the NP242 were used in Hummer H1s and H2s that were more highly rated due to some beefier internal components, and some of them can be retrofitted into the Jeep version. Production of this transfer case straddled New Process's name change to New Venture, but little changed with this transfer case throughout its production run.

The full-time capability of the NP242 made it a very popular option in colder climates with ice and snow, and it has proven to be a very durable transfer case. It has several beefy components, including a 1.25-inch-wide chain and a 6-pinion planetary. It shares the same bolt pattern and spline count as the NP231, making the two transfer cases largely interchangeable and adaptable to a wide variety of manual and automatic transmissions. The one shortcoming of the NP242 among off-road enthusiasts is the lack of an SYE. However, that was solved by Tom Woods Driveshafts, which offers a heavy-duty SYE kit with a 32-spline output shaft.

Identifying Features

From 1987 until the introduction of the JK in 2007, all New Process/New Venture transfer cases looked remarkably similar. Indeed, it's very difficult to differentiate an NP231 and an NP242 externally. Fortunately, most of them have the model number stamped on a red and silver circular tag that has been riveted to the back of the case right in the center.

Jeep TJ/JK NP241OR

The NP241OR (or RockTrac transfer case), which was a game-changer for the capability of 4x4s offered right off the showroom floor, is one of the key components in a Wrangler Rubicon.

Applications and Variations

Introduced in 2003 on the TJ Wrangler and LJ Unlimited, the Rubicon option was a direct response to the growing popularity of off-roading and the public's desire for a more capable 4x4 straight from the factory. The secret sauce of the NP241OR is its 4:1 low range, which is a huge jump in gear reduction over the NP231's 2.72:1 low range. That much gear reduction also means a lot more torque transfer, but the NP241OR has all of the components to handle that with ease. It has proven to be an excellent transfer case, holding up to larger tires, compound gearing, and even V-8 power. It's possible to find the strength limits of the NP241OR, but that's usually only found by extreme off-roaders or heavy abuse. The NP241OR continued into the production of the JK Wrangler in 2007.

Because of its use in later-model, fuel-injected applications, the 2003–2006 versions of the NP241OR have a three-wire vehicle speed sensor (VSS) instead of a mechanical speedometer port. The 2007-and-later versions of the case do not have a VSS because the speed signal is generated from the antilock braking system (ABS). These cases also have a fixed rear output yoke, which is a telltale way to differentiate an NP241OR from an NP231. The TJ version uses conventional yokes, while the JK uses a Rezeppa-style driveshaft that is problematic in lifted applications. Yokes are available to convert the JK transfer cases to a more traditional constant velocity (CV)–style driveshaft.

Identifying Features

As with other New Process/New Venture transfer cases, the NP241OR is easily identified by the circular tag that is riveted to the back of the case. Although the NP241OR is similar in size and shape to a regular NP241 (extensively in GM and Dodge applications), the NP241OR has a different case and several different internal components. Most notably, the front portion of the housing is significantly larger than an NP231 to accommodate the lower gearing inside.

Strength and Swapability

Strength-wise, the NP241OR transfer case is tough and was meant to see extensive off-road use. With the exception of the lack of a mechanical speedometer provision, the NP241OR can be swapped in place of an NP231 with little to no modification.

BorgWarner 1305/1339

The BorgWarner 1305 represented Jeep's first foray into offering a full-time four-wheel-drive system.

Applications and Variations

Introduced in 1973 and continuing through 1979, the unit was marketed as the Quadratrac option alongside traditional part-time systems that used the Dana 20. It was used primarily in Wagoneers and V-8-powered CJs.

Unique in several ways, the BorgWarner 1305/1339 was the first chain-driven case with an aluminum housing that Jeep used. The 1305 offered no low range—only full-time high range and Hi-Lock. Low range (2.57:1) was offered with the 1339 and was achieved with a bolt-on auxiliary reduction box that was positioned on the back of the case next to the rear

Although it is uncommon, this is a BorgWarner 1305 transfer case. It can be identified as such because it doesn't have the large, round low-range housing on the back of the case. Desert racers often used these cases because they offered all-wheel drive but saved weight by not having the low-range gearset, which wasn't needed for racing.

The Quadratrac transfer case doesn't look anything like any other transfer case that Jeep used. This particular one has the large round housing next to the rear output shaft, indicating that this is a 1339 equipped with low range. This one also has an upgraded billet vacuum actuator that replaced the problematic actuator the factory used.

output. Due to the bolt-on nature of the low-range set, a 1305 can be converted to a 1339. The Quadratrac system had the front and rear outputs offset to the passenger's side (like the Dana 18), which required an offset rear differential to match. It was only offered behind the Turbo Hydra-Matic 400 (TH400) automatic transmission.

The Quadratrac system has a checkered reputation. It requires a special fluid to work with its limited-slip friction cone, and using the wrong fluid leads to noise and component failure. It is vacuum operated (usually via a button mounted in the glovebox), which is also problematic. The unit itself is bulky and heavy compared to other transfer cases, and swapping it out for a traditional part-time case requires either installing a Dana 18 or replacing the offset rear axle for a centered one.

Still, when properly maintained, the transfer case is quite strong and was popular among desert racers because of its durability and full-time capability. A part-time conversion kit is available from Mile Marker that does away with the problematic limited-slip center differential, but the conversion process is involved and rather expensive. Replacement parts for these transfer cases are becoming more and more scarce, mostly due to age and the relatively limited production run.

NV147 and NV247/NV249

Introduced with the Grand Cherokee WJ, the NV147 is a rare full-time transfer case with no low range. It was marketed as the Quadratrac I.

The NV247/NV249 was much more common. It was marketed as the Quadratrac II and later the Quadra-Drive system when it was combined with progressive on-demand, limited-slip differentials in the axles. This full-time four-wheel-drive transfer case uses a gerotor coupling to bias torque between the front and rear axles, allegedly providing up to a 50-50 split (when needed) as well as 4-Lo with the center coupler locked.

The fact that there's no locked provision in 4-Hi is suspect, and the jury is still out on how durable the center coupling really is. Although, I must admit that the Quadra-Drive system works pretty slick in factory form. As with other New Venture cases, the model is stamped on the circular identification tag on the back of the transfer case.

JL Wrangler NV241, NV241OR, and MP3022

The introduction of the JL Wrangler in 2018 and the JT Gladiator in 2020 marked another change in Jeep transfer cases with the phasing out of the NP231 in favor of the NV241 in standard models.

Largely the same in terms of specifications as the NP231, the NV241 features a 2.72:1 low range and offers 2-Hi, part-time 4-Hi, and 4-Lo. The NV241 bears a passing resemblance to the NP231, but the case is shaped differently, with ribbing and the absence of the traditional circular identification tag.

The NV241OR Rock-Trac shares the same model designation as the previous TJ and JK Rubicon transfer cases, but it features a different exterior, and I suspect that several internal changes were made as well.

The MP3022 is an option on Sahara models and standard on all Hemi-powered Wranglers. This is an electronically controlled full-time 4WD transfer case that adjusts the torque split between the axles based on several factors, including throttle input and wheel slippage. In addition to full-time operation, the MP3022 has a 4:1 low range.

Unfortunately, none of these transfer cases have an identification tag like the previous New Venture models had. So, the best method of identification is to search the internet for the part number that's engraved on the housing. The front portion of the housing on an NV241OR is significantly larger in diameter than a conventional NV241 to accommodate the larger 4:1 planetary gearset.

Although the MP3022 is still pretty new as of this writing, an alarming number of problems have been reported, mostly related to the full-time 4WD system. It remains to be seen if these problems are electronic or mechanical.

This MP3022 is an all-wheel-drive transfer case that is optional in the Sahara and standard on Hemi-powered JLs. As indicated, it has a full-time 4WD mode as well as a 4:1 low range.

CHAPTER 2

DANA 18 TRANSFER CASE REBUILD

The Dana 18 is a great transfer case, and it helped the Jeep achieve its iconic status among GIs and civilians alike. It's a cast-iron, gear-driven transfer case that uses very simple internals. Therefore, it is one of the easier transfer cases to rebuild, especially if you follow the tips and tricks that are included in this book. A properly serviced Dana 18 should provide years of trouble-free service and is an excellent choice for any classic Jeep.

Any quality Dana 18 rebuild kit includes a new intermediate shaft and bearings. Always replace these parts when doing a rebuild because they are high-wear items.

Tools

If you're diving into a transfer case rebuild, chances are good that you already own an average or above-average number of tools. Rather than focus on every single tool that is needed, I'm focusing on the special or unusual tools that aren't necessarily part of a moderately-equipped toolbox. This includes the following:

- Hydraulic shop press
- Seal puller
- Brass drift
- Snap-ring pliers
- Gasket sealant
- Dial indicator (with magnetic base)
- Permatex Copper Spray-A-Gasket
- Assorted wood blocks
- Calipers
- Dead-blow hammer/brass mallet
- Pressure washer/degreaser/rags/gloves

Intermediate Shafts

Always check the intermediate shaft's outside diameter before purchasing a rebuild kit for your transfer case. The Dana 18 used three different sizes during its production: 3/4 inch (early), 1$^{1}/_{8}$ inches (middle), and 1¼ inches (late). Fortunately, you can determine the intermediate shaft's size without disassembling the case. There is enough of the intermediate shaft (the shaft in the middle of the case) sticking out to measure the intermediate shaft's outside diameter with a set of calipers.

All of these generations of the Dana 18 interchange, and there's no telling what was swapped in or out of the Jeep at some point during its 40- to 80-year life. Don't assume that your CJ-3A has a 1$^{1}/_{8}$-inch shaft. Always measure to be sure.

Rebuild Kits

Be leery of inexpensive rebuild kits. Several inferior overseas-manufactured intermediate shafts are available with poor hardening that will rapidly wear when put into service. Using quality rebuild kits, such as those from

Novak Conversions, is a safe bet and isn't much more expensive than the cheap stuff once you factor in the labor required to replace an inferior shaft. It also helps support an American company with a stellar reputation for quality.

This chapter covers the disassembly, inspection, and reassembly procedures. Take careful notes and photos during disassembly so that you know how parts are oriented and how they should be reassembled. The critical information is provided to make your rebuild a success, but the success of the rebuild ultimately depends on your attention to detail.

Have what you need on hand to do the teardown and rebuild within a reasonable amount of time. Waiting weeks, months, or even years between disassembly and reassembly inevitably leads to confusion and frustration.

I used the master rebuild kit from Novak Conversions. I consider Novak Conversions to be *the* source for transfer-case knowledge and parts. Novak Conversions is known for high-quality parts and great customer service. It is the only trustworthy source for intermediate shafts with proper hardening, and the company even provides O-rings on the shafts to minimize leaks. Novak Conversions also offers several parts upgrades, including an O-ring output-shaft bearing cap and an extra-capacity inspection cover for the Dana 18.

A quality rebuild kit, such as this one from Novak Conversions, includes everything that is shown from bearings to gaskets to shims and small parts. Rebuilding a transfer case is not the easiest job to tackle, so why settle for a cheap incomplete kit or one with poor quality components? Do it right and do it once.

Scan this QR code with your smartphone to view the Novak Conversion Dana 18 rebuild kit.

Disassembling a Dana 18 Transfer Case

1 ***The Dana 18 is married to the transmission, and separating it is a little unconventional. Behind the five-bolt PTO cover is a gear that is retained with a large nut and cotter pin. That nut is actually installed on the output shaft of the transmission, so the nut and the main drive gear needs to be removed before the transfer case can be separated from the transmission. If the Jeep is equipped with an overdrive or a PTO, additional steps are required to remove those components, and the retention method is not a conventional nut.***

Disassembling a Dana 18 Transfer Case *continued*

2 *After the nut and drive gear are removed, the transfer case can be separated from the transmission. Five 3/8-inch bolts attach the transfer case to the transmission. It's particularly easy to miss the one that is closest to the intermediate shaft because it's usually buried under grease and grime. Take precautions to keep the transmission's output shaft seated forward (toward the front of the transmission) as you separate the two cases. If it backs out, several ball bearings will fall to the bottom of the transmission, necessitating a partial disassembly of the transmission to put the bearings back in place. The front bearing may or may not stay in the transfer case. It's fine either way, as it can be removed later if needed.*

3 *As with all rebuilds, it's worth taking the time to hose off the exterior of the case as much as possible. There is usually a lot of build up with multiple decades of grease and grime. Getting the outside reasonably clean makes for a better overall experience. This transfer case has had multiple sessions with a pressure washer and degreaser, so it was really nasty before I started.*

4 *To remove the parking brake assembly, remove the rear output shaft nut and the rear output drive flange. The remaining portions of the assembly are held in place with four bolts. You can rebuild the parking brake assembly if you choose, or you can remove it permanently if you want, as it does not impact the operation of the transfer case. If you choose to not use the parking brake, swap the factory output flange for a conventional 1310 yoke (Spicer part number 2-4-2851X). In this case, I opted to not reinstall the parking brake.*

5 *A bolt holding the retaining plate for the intermediate shaft is on the back side of the case. Remove this as well as the bottom inspection cover. Using a brass drift, tap the intermediate shaft rearward (toward the rear output shaft) out of the case. Do not attempt to drive it out forward. If you do, you will damage the case. You may hear a bunch of needle bearings fall as you drive the intermediate shaft out. Don't worry. Retrieve them from the bottom of the case later. Once it's out, lift out the intermediate gear along with its shims and roller bearings.*

Disassembling a Dana 18 Transfer Case *continued*

6 ***Remove the four bolts holding the rear output housing to the main case. There are several shims positioned between the housing and the case. Be sure to save these! Those shims will be important later.***

7 ***There are two hex-head caps on either side of the front output housing in line with the shift rails. These hold the spring and poppet ball for each shift rail. Remove the caps, springs, and poppet balls. Save all of these parts, as not all rebuild kits include new springs and poppet balls. Engage front-wheel drive by pulling the left shift rail (the one closest to the center of the transfer case) forward. (Have the end of the rail as far out of the case as it will go.) Place all small parts in a bag and label them to ease potential confusion during reassembly.***

8 *Remove the bolts that secure the front output housing to the case. Tap it with a mallet to break it loose and remove it as an assembly with the front output shaft, shifter clutch shift collar, shift fork, and shift rod. Be careful not to lose the interlock pill once the front housing is removed.*

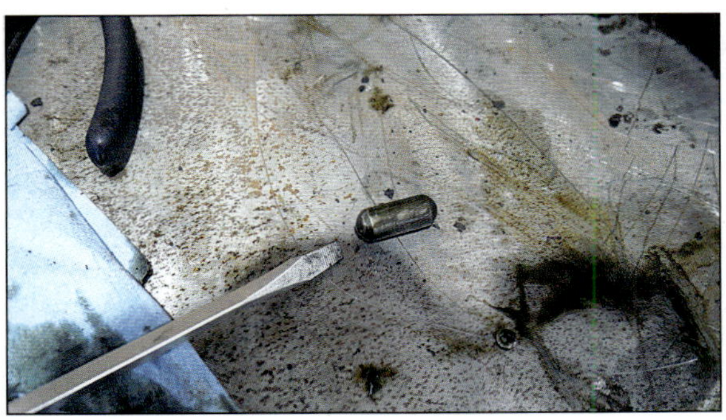

9 *This is the interlock pill. It prevents the transfer case from getting shifted into low range until the transfer case is first shifted into 4WD. The problem with this is that many drivers may find it very handy to be in low range while still being in 2WD. In other transfer cases, the interlock pill is very important, but with the Dana 18, it really doesn't serve much of a purpose, as no damage can be done to the case by removing it. If the Jeep is going to spend time off-road, I recommend removing it, as 2-Low can be useful in a variety of situations.*

10 ***After the front output is removed, use a mallet or brass drift to tap the rear output shaft rearward and unseat the bearing race and bearing from the rear of the case. This provides enough room to address the front bearing. Use a large screwdriver between the front bearing and the output gear to move the bearing forward on the shaft and thus expose the snap ring (arrow) holding the output gear to the shaft. Don't pry against the gear or you may end up chipping a tooth on the gear. Use snap-ring pliers to unseat the snap ring from the groove in the output shaft and slide the snap ring forward on the shaft. Once it is unseated, the shaft can be slid out of the gear and removed from the rear of the case.***

11 *Sometimes the rear output bearing for the rear output shaft can be removed by striking the end of the output shaft on a block of wood, but sometimes it's a bit more stubborn, as was the case with this one. If that method doesn't work, use a bearing puller and a shop press to press off the bearing (as shown). The new bearing can be installed in a similar manner, or you can use a piece of tubing slightly larger than the outside diameter of the shaft to tap the new bearing into place. Only press on the inner race of the bearing. Pressing on the outer race will damage the bearing.*

12 *The last piece of the puzzle is disassembling the front output housing, which contains the front input shaft, the 4WD shift rail and collar, and the front output seals. Usually, these are in pretty good shape—unless the Jeep has been used extensively in 4WD or is not equipped with locking hubs. Still, replace the front output bearing as well as the shift seals. The shift rail and fork can simply be pulled out of the housing, exposing the internal snap ring that holds the front bearing in the housing. Use a screwdriver to remove the snap ring, and then the bearing and shaft can be removed from the housing. Remove the shift rail seals with a seal puller or a large screwdriver.*

13 *The only remaining item for disassembly is to remove the Hi-Lo shift rail and fork. It's possible to leave these in place, but it is very difficult to install the front output housing without damaging the seal on the recesses on the end of the rail. To remove it, note the orientation of the fork in relation to the rail. Then, remove the set screw from the fork and remove the rail from the housing. Sometimes, this set screw it secured with safety wire, as it was in this case. Make note of how the wire was installed so that you can replicate the orientation with new safety wire.*

14 ***One of the most tedious aspects of rebuilding an old transfer case is cleaning all of the components, but cleanliness is critical to a successful rebuild. If you have access to one, an industrial parts washer is invaluable and makes the process much quicker and easier. Otherwise, a home parts washer filled with mineral spirits or a similar solvent does the job. I soaked all of the components in a home parts washer for several days and spent a lot of time with a wire brush on the case and other exterior components. Aside from using an industrial parts washer, it's not going to be perfect, but getting everything as clean as you can leads to a more satisfactory outcome and makes it easier to inspect everything, which should be done before proceeding any further.***

After disassembly is complete, there are several items to check to ensure that the components you have are serviceable and can be reused.

With a transfer case as old as the Dana 18, it is nearly impossible to find a perfect example. Items such as case cracks and bent forks inevitably lead to leaks, frustration, and a transfer case that doesn't function properly. Chipped or badly pitted teeth from water contamination are also common. Take the time to make a thorough inspection.

Fortunately, parts for these transfer cases are readily available. However, be leery of buying brand-new components unless they are NOS. Many overseas replacement parts are inferior quality and have questionable hardness that will cause wear and premature failure. I'd lean toward sourcing serviceable used parts instead of purchasing new parts if something must be replaced. I am assuming that you will already be replacing all of the bearings with a quality rebuild kit. Reusing bearings in a case that is as old as a Dana 18 is never a good idea.

Inspecting a Disassembled Dana 18 Transfer Case

1 *Inspect the main case very carefully. Because of the loads that are placed on the case, hairline cracks can develop. It's common to find hairline cracks that run from the intermediate shaft bores to the bottom cover surface. I've also seen cracks near the rear output shaft bore, but these are usually the result of a catastrophic failure, such as breaking the output shaft. If present, these cracks are usually hairline cracks that can be very difficult to detect. Inspecting the inside and outside of the case is useful. If you find a case crack, replace the case. Repairing a cracked case takes highly specialized skills and equipment, and the results are rarely satisfactory. The cracks often return.*

2 *Inspect all of the bearing surfaces on the front and rear output shafts as well as the bore of the intermediate gear. Any signs of galling indicate that the bearing has spun on the shaft and that the shaft should be replaced. Also, inspect the splines for any chips or twists that could impact gear engagement or movement. On the front output shaft (shown), inspect the end of the shaft that engages the rear output shaft for evidence of galling, indicating that the transfer case was run low on oil.*

3 *Inspect the bronze bushing in the end of the output shaft and measure its inside diameter with a pair of calipers. The specification when new is 0.628 inch. Anything above 0.630 inch is excessive, and the bushing should be replaced. If needed, this is best done by a machine shop, as the bushing must be pressed into place and then reamed to the proper inside diameter. Often, it's cheaper and easier to simply source a new output shaft if the bushing is damaged or out of spec.*

Inspecting a Disassembled Dana 18 Transfer Case *continued*

4 *Inspect both shift forks for straightness. The fork should be at a perfect 90-degree angle in relation to the shift rails. A bent fork causes hard shifting and a transfer case that jumps out of gear.*

5 *Carefully inspect all of the gears for cracked, chipped, missing, or excessively pitted teeth. Cracked or missing teeth are a no-go; get a new gear. Pitting is another story. There will be some evidence of water contamination in just about every Dana 18 that is taken apart. It's how severe that pitting is that is something of a judgement call. This is the input gear that came out of my transfer case, and I was on the fence about replacing it. While it wasn't ideal, I chose to keep it because 1) the transfer case ran quiet before removal, 2) it's not a daily driver, and 3) a pitted used gear will probably still work better than an overseas-manufactured new one. Most of the Jeeps that use these transfer cases are not primary drivers. They are weekend cruisers that rarely see sustained freeway speeds. Half-rotted-away teeth are one thing, but some pitting on the face of the gears is another. Use your own judgement and weigh the use and goals for the Jeep to determine the best course for your needs and budget.*

Reassembling a Dana 18 Transfer Case

1 *It's time to begin reassembly. Removing the original transfer case seals is difficult without a seal puller, so invest in the tool if you don't already own one. The puller is also handy for removing the front and rear output seals. To avoid leaks, take precautions to avoid scoring the bores for the seals. Installing the new seals is straightforward. Tap them in with a socket that has close to the same outside diameter as the seals.*

2 *Press a new bearing on the rear of the rear output shaft and on the front of the front output shaft. If you took apart the front housing, reinstall the front output and gear assembly and secure it with the snap ring that was present during disassembly. Remove any rust or pitting from both shift rails with an emery cloth. Lightly grease and install the shorter of the two rails from the front in the left shift-rail bore (the farthest to the outside of the case once it is assembled). Slide the 4WD shift collar on the rail and secure it using the original set screw and safety wire if needed. The thick end of the collar faces rearward.*

3 *Turn the front output housing on its side and insert the interlock pill (if desired) into the spring and poppet ball hole. Lightly grease the longer of the two shift rails (the Hi-Lo rail) and install it from the front. Installing both rails from the front prevents damaging the new shift-rail seals with the machined detents on the front of the rails that engage the shifters. The 4WD shift rail needs to be all the way forward for the interlock pill to drop far enough to install the Hi-Lo rail. Install and tighten the set screw and safety wire (if applicable) of the Hi-Lo shift rail.*

4 *The gasket thickness of the front output housing plays a role in output-shaft endplay, which is measured later. Therefore, it's necessary to install the front output bearing race in the case as well as the housing itself with the shift rails, gasket, and gasket sealant (I highly recommend) as an assembly. As the front output housing is inserted on the case, slide the Hi-Lo shift fork on the rail because it can't be done once the front housing is in place. The thick end of the fork faces forward (as shown). Install and torque the front output housing bolts to 23 ft-lbs. Install and tighten the set screw and safety wire (if applicable) of the Hi-Lo shift rail.*

5 *With the front output shaft assembly secured, install the rear output shaft along with the output-shaft gear and sliding gear. This is another step where the order of assembly is important. Insert the output shaft (with the rear bearing already installed) partially into the main housing. Then, position the sliding gear with the shift collar facing rearward and engage the collar with the shift fork. Install the output gear, followed by the spacer, the new snap ring, and the bearing. The order of assembly is shown here. Each part must be installed together and in sequence.*

6 *This is another view of the correct orientation of the gears on the main shaft.*

Reassembling a Dana 18 Transfer Case *continued*

7 ***After everything is in, seat the snap ring for the front bearing. Walk it back until it positively seats in the output-shaft groove. Then, lightly tap the rear output shaft forward to seat the front bearing as well as the rear bearing race.***

8 ***With the front and rear output shafts installed, there's another critical step: measuring output-shaft endplay. Endplay is adjusted via shims (right) installed between the output-shaft bearing cap and the main case. Begin with the initial shim thickness, which you can measure after cleaning the original shims. Add 0.010 inch to the initial thickness, which may require combining shims from the old shim pack and new ones included in your rebuild kit. If you don't have the original shims, you can get an approximation by dry-fitting the rear bearing housing and using a feeler gauge to measure the gap between the output cap and the case.***

9 *Install the rear output bearing cap with the shim pack (again, dry-fit) and torque the bearing-cap bolts to 30 ft-lbs. Using a mallet, tap the rear output shaft forward. Then, firmly tap the rear output housing (not the shaft) rearward. This seats the bearing races in their respective housings to obtain an accurate endplay measurement. This is the only way to get an accurate reading. Place a dial indicator on the output shaft as shown and measure the endplay. The factory specification is 0.004–0.008 inch, but according to Novak, better results are achieved by aiming for 0.002 to 0.006 inch. If you need to change shims, reseat the rear output bearing race each time a change is made to achieve an accurate measurement.*

10 *After proper shim thickness and endplay is achieved, permanently attach the rear output bearing housing to the case. The shim pack is an integral part of sealing the case, as oil travels to the rear bearing housing. There are different schools of thought regarding sealing. There are a variety of old-school sealing methods, but I've had the best luck by carefully cleaning each shim to be sure it's free of oil and then applying a light coat of Permatex's Copper Spray-A-Gasket to each side of each shim. I apply the sealer and let it get tacky before lining them up for final installation. I've had poor luck with conventional RTV sealers.*

Reassembling a Dana 18 Transfer Case *continued*

11 *Install the speedometer drive gear before the final installation of the rear output housing. The correct orientation is shown, with the thick end of the gear pointing forward. Once positioned, apply any final sealer and torque the rear output bearing cap to 30 ft-lbs.*

12 *Another old-school versus new-school predicament is with the output-shaft yoke seals. The replacement seals that typically come with a rebuild kit mimic the originals: a single rubber-lip seal with a felt outer (right). I'm guessing that they knew the rubber seal would leak and hoped that the felt would help slow it down. Some people report excellent luck with using modern seals (National part number 473229) and using two of them per output. There's an added benefit that the new seals don't ride where the original did on the yoke, so there's less chance of surface contamination. Since I knew the originals were going to leak, I opted for trying the newer seals and doubled them up. (You'll need a total of four for both outputs.) So far, so good.*

13 *Whether you install the original seals or the National seals, drive the first rubber seal all the way to the bottom of the bore. It is followed by the felt seal (or the second National if you so choose). Then, reinstall the yokes, torque them to 110 ft-lbs, and install new cotter pins if applicable.*

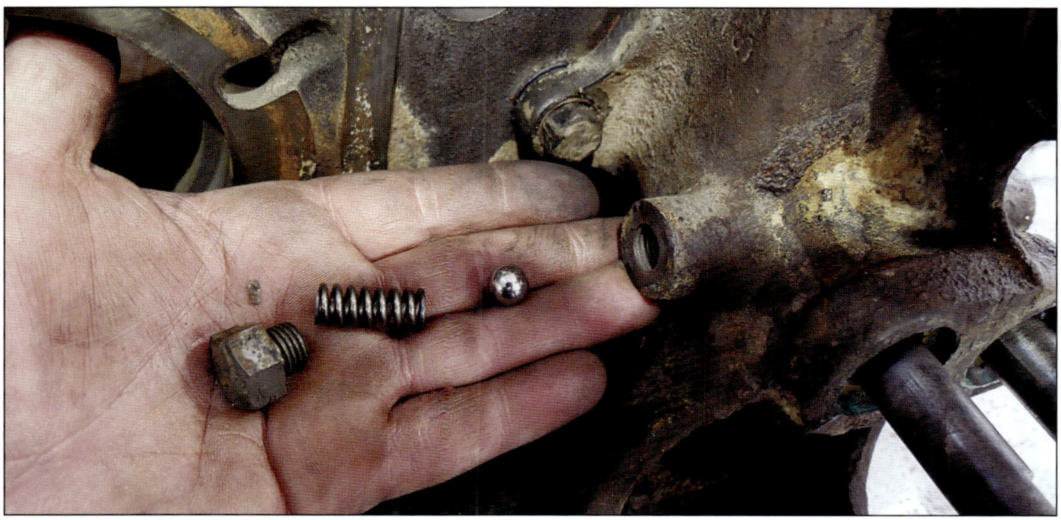

14 *Install the new poppet balls and springs that should be included with your rebuild kit and retain them using the original caps on the outside of each shift rail.*

15 ***The last piece of the puzzle is installing the intermediate gear, thrust washers, bearings, and the intermediate shaft. The 3/4- and 1 1/8-inch intermediate shafts have caged roller bearings that make installation fairly easy. The 1 1/4-inch shafts use uncaged rollers that must be stacked in the bore of the intermediate gear. A Novak intermediate shaft (shown here) has the added bonus of two O-rings on each end of the shaft to help reduce leaks. Use an engine assembly lube or frozen petroleum jelly (Vaseline) to lightly grease the gears, bore, and shaft. Avoid using heavier grease. Use something that will assist with initial lubrication and then melt into the gear oil instead of repelling it like wheel bearing grease will. Stacking uncaged bearings is tedious and tricky, but using a healthy amount of assembly lube helps to hold things in place during assembly.***

16 *Installing the intermediate gear requires finesse and possibly a few attempts to be successful, especially with uncaged bearings. Begin by using assembly lube to "glue" the thrust washers to the inside of the case. Then, carefully lower the gear into position. Insert the intermediate shaft from the rear only and drive it toward the front of the case. When you get within about 3/4 inch of the shaft being seated, make sure that it's rotated properly to accept the retaining plate and bolt before driving it all the way home. If you're using a Novak shaft, don't forget to install the O-rings.*

17 *Check your work. Shift the transfer case into all of its ranges to ensure that everything rotates smoothly when it's supposed to and doesn't bind up. If there's any issue, address it now. The only items left to install are the bottom inspection cover and PTO cover. I use a sealant called Great Stuff instead of conventional RTV. It tends to do a much better job sealing these old cases as long as everything is clean and dry.*

CHAPTER 3

Dana 20 Transfer Case Rebuild

The Dana 20 had an extremely long production run and was used in a wide variety of Jeep models. It also saw widespread usage with International as well as Ford with the first-generation Bronco.

Jeep Dana 20s were largely consistent throughout their production run, with only an outer-shaft spline-count change from 10 to 26. The same cannot be said of the shifter arrangements among the various Jeep models. The Dana 20 has no direct provisions for mounting the shifters, and due to its use behind engines and transmissions of various lengths and models with different seating positions, the shifter arrangements were often strange, convoluted, and problematic. For this reason, a twin-stick conversion is a common and popular upgrade.

The Dana 20 resembles both the Dana 18 and the Dana 300, but the best telltale clues to identify a Dana 20 are the centered rear output (as opposed to offset) and the cast-iron front and rear output housings. The Dana 20 is an excellent transfer case overall. Its biggest shortcoming is the measly 2:1 low-range ratio, but that can be improved with an aftermarket gearset.

The Dana 20 shares the "backward Texas" five-bolt pattern with the Dana 18 and has a similar input gear arrangement where the input gear is retained on the output shaft of the transmission. This makes many Dana 20s interchangeable with Dana 18s (at least the manual versions), but it also means that you need to be sure to grab the input gear from the back of the transmission if you're obtaining one from a donor vehicle to build.

Tools

If you're rebuilding a transfer case, chances are good that you already own the average number of tools, including wrenches, sockets, screwdrivers, etc. Rather than focus on every single tool that is needed, I'm focusing on the special or unusual tools that aren't necessarily part of a moderately-equipped toolbox. This includes the following:

- $1^{1}/_{16}$- or $1^{1}/_{8}$-inch socket
- Brass drift
- Dead-blow hammer/brass mallet
- Hydraulic shop press
- Dial indicator (with magnetic base)
- Calipers
- Assorted wood blocks
- Pencil torch/methylacetylene-propadiene propane (MAPP)
- Air hammer
- Parts washer/pressure washer
- Assorted rags and cleaners
- Sandwich bags to identify/label small parts

Durability

The Dana 20 is an extremely durable transfer case, capable of standing up to V-8 power and big tires. The low range is a bit disappointing (only 2.03:1), but it can be improved by swapping in gears from a Bronco Dana 20 that yields a 2.46:1 ratio or by using aftermarket gears that drop to a much more rock-crawling-friendly 3.15:1.

In addition, it's only 10½ inches long from the face of the front case to the output-shaft yoke, which makes it an extremely compact unit. It offers much quieter operation than the Dana 18 due to the rear output being centered and a direct drive from the input. Overall, there's very little reason to change out a Dana 20 in any application that had one from the factory, even when a powerful engine is used.

Problems

As with the Dana 18, the biggest enemies to a Dana 20 are case cracks and water intrusion. The Dana 20 shares gear oil with the transmission, and water frequently gets into a transmission via the shifter cane on open-topped vehicles.

Case cracks are somewhat less common, but they do happen, so it's important to closely inspect the case and the internals of a Dana 20 during teardown. If case cracks are found, source a new case, as it's nearly impossible to repair a crack permanently. Attempts to do so usually just lead to more cracks.

Light pitting on the gears usually isn't a problem and can often be polished out, but major pitting seriously compromises overall strength and leads to excessive noise.

As with the other Dana transfer cases, there aren't many specialized tools that are required to rebuild a Dana 20. For the most part, common hand tools are all that is needed. However, a shop press is handy, and a dial indicator with a magnetic base is required to properly measure endplay.

Rebuild Kits

Dana 20 rebuild kits are available from a variety of sources. However, as with the Dana 18, many overseas-sourced rebuild kits have inferior bearings and intermediate shafts that haven't been hardened properly. In addition, not all of them are 100-percent complete.

Using a rebuild kit from a reputable company, such as Novak Conversions or Advance Adapters, is a safe bet. I obtained the rebuild kit that was used in this chapter from Advance Adapters. The only part that wasn't included was an intermediate shaft. Replacing the intermediate shaft isn't quite as critical as on a Dana 18, but it's still a good practice and should be considered as a mandatory part of any quality rebuild. I sourced a new shaft from Novak Conversions.

Disassembling and Inspecting a Dana 20 Transfer Case

1 *Begin the disassembly by pulling the front and rear output yokes, which are retained by a $1^1/_{16}$- or $1^1/_8$-inch nut, depending on the case. It's usually necessary to tap these yokes off of the shafts after the nut has been removed. Early Dana 20s had 10-spline output shafts, while the later versions had 26-spline shafts. Standard 1310 yokes (as well as larger 1330 and 1350 yokes) are available for both spline counts. Although, they are more common for the later ones.*

2 *As with the Dana 18 and Dana 300, the Dana 20 has a large, stamped-steel inspection cover on the bottom. Pop the cover on any Dana 20 before buying or rebuilding. Water intrusion is a common issue because Dana 20s share oil with the transmission, and water often gets in through the transmission shifter. This one looked good at first but later revealed some water damage. Also, look for chipped teeth and signs of excessive wear.*

3 *The intermediate shaft in the center of the case is held in place by a lock plate that is retained by a 5/16-inch bolt on the back of the case near the rear output housing. Remove the bolt and lock plate but save them for reuse.*

4 *Use a brass punch to drive the intermediate shaft rearward out of the case. Do not drive the shaft out forward; the shaft is machined to be slightly larger in the rear, so attempting to drive it out forward can damage the case. Don't be alarmed if you hear a whole bunch of needle bearings fall inside the case. This is normal. The intermediate shaft is a common wear point and should always be replaced during a rebuild.*

Disassembling and Inspecting a Dana 20 Transfer Case *continued*

5 *Once the shaft is removed, lift out the large intermediate gear through the inspection-cover hole. Inside the gear are some spacers and a bunch of loose roller bearings, some of which probably fell into the case. There are also a pair of thrust washers that can be removed. Unbeknownst to me, someone had been in this case recently, and the rollers were still packed with grease in the intermediate gear bore.*

6 *Remove the five bolts that attach the rear output housing to the case and separate the housing from the main case. It will come out with the rear output shaft, which is fine. Avoid the urge to stick a screwdriver between the rear output and the main housing to pry them apart. Doing so damages the seal surface and causes leaks. A few radial taps with a rubber mallet is usually sufficient to knock the housing loose.*

7 *Press the rear output shaft into the rear outer bearing. You can use a shop press to push the output shaft forward and out of the housing. Alternatively, you can also use an air hammer with a pointed tip to push the shaft out. Both methods are equally effective, but it's a good idea to partially reinstall the nut in both cases to avoid damaging the threads on the tip of the shaft.*

8 *With the rear output separated from the housing, you can see the inner bearing that is also pressed on the shaft, the speedometer drive gear, and some shims (arrows). These shims are very important! They control the endplay adjustment of the output shaft, so make careful note of these shims and put them in a safe place.*

Disassembling and Inspecting a Dana 20 Transfer Case *continued*

9 *Back at the main case, remove the four-bolt cap on the back of the case that retains the rear bearing race for the front output shaft. The shims under this cap control endplay for the front output shaft and are very important. Be sure to save these shims because they will be needed later.*

10 *Inside the case is the shift fork for the rear output shaft. It's retained on the shift rail by a set screw. Remove this set screw, and you can manipulate the fork enough to remove the shift collar that engages the fork out of the case. Be careful not to strip out the set screw. Sometimes, applying some heat to the fork loosens up the thread-locking compound that was likely used to hold it in place.*

11 *Tap the front output shaft rearward enough to unseat the rear bearing race from the case. The entire front output-shaft assembly can now be slid rearward (as shown). Shift the Hi/Lo fork rearward as far as it will go in the case so that the gear that engages the fork is resting against the rear wall of the main case.*

12 *The front output-shaft bearing is pressed onto the output shaft and must be separated to remove the output shaft from the case. With older cases, there is a thrust washer between the bearing and the gear that you can pry against enough to slide the bearing forward and reveal a snap ring that can be removed (similar to the Dana 18). This was a later unit without the snap ring. With the large gear resting against the back wall of the main case (not the shift fork), use a punch or an air hammer to drive the bearing off the shaft. The bearing has a light press fit and should come off relatively easily. Once it is free, remove the shaft from the rear of the case. Then, lift out the remaining gears.*

13 *For reference, this shows the order of disassembly and assembly of the front output shaft for a later Dana 20 transfer case. The thick washer and thinner washer sandwich the front output shaft bearing. It's important to get the position of these spacers correct to obtain proper endplay.*

14 *Remove the caps or 4WD-indicator switch out of the top of the shift-rail housing. Flip the transfer case upside down and place a rag underneath the shift tower. Twist the shift rail closest to the input/rear output opening in the case 90 degrees with a screwdriver. Pull the rail outward toward the front of the case. It may be necessary to reposition the other shift rail inward or outward to allow the interlock pill to drop away from the rod being pulled. Eventually, the poppet ball and spring will fly out of the hole that you removed the plug from, and with any luck, the rag that you positioned under the housing will catch them.*

15 *Note that the fork, spring, and poppet ball are positioned how they will be in the case. Try not to lose these, and hopefully they didn't go flying. Also, note the rust on the shift rail. Clean up any rust or pitting with a wire wheel to give the shift-rail seals a fighting chance of not leaking.*

16 *With the first shift rail out of the way, rotate the remaining shift fork in the case and expose its set screw. The set screw might also be retained with safety wire. Take precautions to not strip out the set screw. If needed, apply some heat to the fork to loosen any thread-locking compound that may have been used. Once loose, pull the remaining shift rail out of the case, being mindful of the poppet ball and spring.*

Disassembling and Inspecting a Dana 20 Transfer Case *continued*

17 *Remove the bolts for the front output housing and remove the remaining races and seals. Clean and inspect everything for excessive wear, damaged teeth or seal surfaces, and case cracks.*

Reassembling a Dana 20 Transfer Case

1 *The front output housing can be assembled multiple ways. Either install the shift fork and rail on the housing first (as I did), or install the rail in the front output housing with the poppet ball and spring and then line up the fork in the case as you install the output and rail assembly together. Regardless of the method that you choose, install the fork as shown, with the thicker end that has the set screw toward the front of the case. Line up the fork's set screw hole with the indentation in the rail. Use a dab of thread-locking compound on the set screw and tighten firmly. Then, rotate the fork into its proper position.*

2 *Install a new bearing on the rear end of the front output shaft. Position the large front output-shaft sliding gear in the case and engage the collar of the gear on the shift fork. This is followed by the smaller front output-shaft gear, which is positioned as shown, with the taller portion of the gear toward the front of the case. Then, install the front output shaft in the case from the rear (sliding it through the two gears in the case) and install the rear bearing cup in the case.*

Reassembling a Dana 20 Transfer Case *continued*

3 *Install the larger of the two spacers on the front output shaft. This is followed by the bearing and the second (smaller) spacer. Again, these spacers are critically important for getting endplay correct. Older models may have a slightly different arrangement with a thrust washer and a snap ring.*

4 *Position the case on its back (as shown). Be sure that the back of the output shaft is supported and not resting on the shift fork. Use a brass punch or a piece of tubing to seat the front bearing for the front output shaft. Again, be certain that the shaft is supported by something other than the shift fork. The bearing has a light press fit and shouldn't take much effort to seat it. Once seated, install the bearing race in the case.*

5 *Prepare the front output housing with a new gasket and a light coating of RTV sealant around the gasket surface of the housing and the main case. Install the spring and poppet ball in the housing and align it with the shift rail. Use a screwdriver to depress the poppet ball enough to slide the shift rail through the housing bore. This can take patience and an extra set of hands. Carefully slide the rail through the seal and continue sliding the housing into place until it's seated against the case. Tighten the bolts to 30 ft-lbs.*

6 *Tap the rear bearing cup forward to seat the front bearing and race. Install the rear bearing cap enough so that it's seated against the bearing cup but not applying much pressure to it. Use a feeler gauge to measure the gap between the bearing cap and the main case. Add 0.010 inch to this number for the trial shim-pack thickness. The shims come in thicknesses of 0.003 inch, 0.010 inch, and 0.031 inch. Install trial shims or start with the old shim-pack thickness. Torque the cap bolts to 30 ft-lbs. Use a block of wood and a hammer to firmly tap on the rear cap to seat the rear bearing cup.*

7 *Using a dial indicator with a magnetic base, measure the amount of endplay on the front output. The correct specification is 0.002 to 0.005 inch of endplay. Add or remove shims to obtain the proper amount of endplay. Note that failing to seat the rear bearing is a common occurrence and can cause people to add a large number of shims in search of the correct endplay. That's not the right way to do it. In most cases, you should end up with no more than three or four shims to achieve the correct amount of endplay.*

8 *Once endplay has been set, seal up the rear bearing cup, which is a common source of leaks. I failed to take a photo of sealing the rear shim pack, but it's essentially the same as a Dana 300 shim pack (shown). Spray each side of each shim with Permatex Copper Spray-A-Gasket along with the bearing cap. Let the copper tack up a bit and then install the shims and cap. Torque to 30 ft-lbs and check endplay one final time.*

9 *Moving on, install the other shift rail with its spring and poppet ball partially in the shift rail housing. Position the rear sliding gear and shift fork in the case, with the collar on the gear facing the rear output hole and engaged on the fork. Tap the shift rail inward and engage the fork on the rail. Align the indent in the rail with the fork's set-screw hole and install the set screw with a dab of threadlocker. Reinstall safety wire if it was present during disassembly.*

10 ***Press a new inner bearing on the rear output shaft (if not done already) and install new races in the rear output-shaft housing. The order of assembly for the rear output shaft and housing is shown. Note the position of the speedometer drive gear as well as the small shims that adjust output-shaft endplay. Begin with the same shim thickness that was there during disassembly.***

11 ***Rear output shaft endplay can be measured on a bench and not attached to the case, but I found it easiest to just install it with a new gasket and RTV sealant. Install the outer bearing and rear yoke, and torque the yoke nut to 140 ft-lbs. Use a dial indicator to measure endplay. The proper specification is 0.003 to 0.006 inch of endplay. Removing shims reduces endplay, and adding shims increases it. If shim changes are needed, remove the yoke and use an air hammer on the shaft to unseat the outer bearing. Once endplay is achieved, install the pinion seal, yoke, and nut, and torque a final time.***

12 *I mentioned water contamination as being a common problem with many of these older cases. The intermediate gear on the right came out of the case, and about half of the teeth were deeply pitted due to prolonged water exposure. I opted to replace it with a good used gear (left) that I sourced online. Some rebuild sources, such as Novak Conversions, have a limited stock of NOS or used gears. Otherwise, online sources, such as eBay, are often the best bet.*

13 *Assemble the uncaged rollers and spacers in the intermediate gear. There are two rows of 24 rollers (for a total of 48) separated by a spacer in the center, and a spacer on the outside of each row of rollers (for a total of three spacers). Use frozen petroleum jelly or engine assembly lube to "glue" the rollers and spacers into place and help hold them in position during final assembly. Avoid using wheel-bearing grease, as it doesn't tend to melt into the gear lube like petroleum jelly or engine assembly lube.*

14 *Two thrust washers sandwich the intermediate gear when it is installed in the case. These can be held in place or "glued" to the inside of the case with assembly lube. Always use new intermediate gear rollers and a new shaft during a rebuild (both are a common source of wear in these cases). Avoid cheap, imported intermediate-shaft kits because they typically have poor hardening and often fail within just a few thousand miles. Sticking with a reputable brand of rebuild kit is always the best bet.*

Reassembling a Dana 20 Transfer Case *continued*

15 ***Carefully position the intermediate gear in the case between the thrust washers. Looping a piece of baling wire around the gear can serve as a handle to help hold it in position as you install the intermediate shaft. Lightly lube the shaft, install it from the rear, and carefully tap it forward. Keep an eye on the opposite end of the bore to be sure that none of the rollers become dislodged.***

16 ***Before fully seating the intermediate shaft, rotate it so that the recess in the shaft lines up with where the small retaining plate will be positioned. Seat the shaft flush with the case and install the retaining plate and bolt.***

17 ***Check your work by shifting the transfer case into all of its gears and check for smooth operation. Install the inspection cover plate with a new gasket and RTV sealant (I use Permatex's The Right Stuff). Avoid the urge to over-torque the bolts. They only need about 15 ft-lbs and should be tightened roughly in a star pattern. Excessive torque can cause the inspection cover to warp and create leaks.***

CHAPTER 4

S-A DESIGN

Dana 300 Transfer Case Rebuild

Transfer-case design evolved from the Dana 18 to the Dana 20, and the same can be said from the Dana 20 to the Dana 300. Although the Dana 300 had a short production run compared to its predecessors, it's better in almost every way.

A deeper low range and modern, more powerful engines required the case to have additional strength, so nearly every component of the Dana 300 is beefier than its predecessors. In addition, the Dana 300 was produced during a time when fuel economy and weight were growing concerns, so this cast-iron case is the first one of the three that had aluminum output housings rather than cast iron to reduce weight. Although it's still heavier than the earlier cases, the extra strength of the Dana 300 more than makes up for the negligible weight difference.

If you have a Dana 300, consider yourself lucky because it's a fantastic and strong transfer case. It's most easily identified by a 6-bolt round input pattern, internal 23-spline input gear, aluminum rear output housing, and an aluminum front output housing/shift tower.

Case Cracks

Even with the extensive use of aluminum, the core of the Dana 300 is cast iron and gear driven, which is one of the reasons it's so strong. However, that cast-iron case has its drawbacks, the biggest of which is cracks. Inspect the case carefully, especially if the transfer case has experienced any type of failure, such as a broken output shaft or internal gear breakage. Often, the stress and shock-load of sudden component failures can cause hairline cracks to develop in the case. Most notably, this may occur in the inspection-cover opening, the bores for the intermediate shaft, and especially in the bore for the rear output-shaft housing.

Unfortunately, if cracks are found, there's almost no chance of fixing the case. Once cracks develop in cast iron, it's nearly impossible to make them stop, and cracks leak. If you find cracks, the best thing to do is source a new case. This is also why it's important to inspect a Dana 300 carefully before purchasing one, especially if the case has an unknown history.

Rebuild Kits

Although it's still relatively straightforward, rebuilding a Dana 300 is more complex than the Dana 20 or Dana 18. There are more press-fit bearings than in previous models, and the overall tolerances are tighter. In addition, special tools are required, including the following items:

- Brass punch/drift
- Dead-blow hammer/brass mallet
- Hydraulic shop press
- Dial indicator with magnetic base
- Calipers
- Assorted wood blocks
- Pencil torch/MAPP
- Snap-ring pliers
- Gasket sealant
- 1$^1/_8$-inch socket

The teardown and reassembly steps must be followed in a specific order, and it can be confusing at times as to what needs to happen next. While I recommend that first-timers begin with one of the other transfer cases covered in this book, a beginner with an above-average attention to detail and patience can tackle the project with success. If you've never rebuilt a Dana 300 before, I recommend reading through this procedure a few times as well as any instructions that come with your rebuild kit prior to starting the project.

As with so many of the other transfer cases in this book, good rebuild kits are available as well as some very poor ones. A rebuild kit is not a place to cut corners and save a few dollars. Rebuilding a transfer case requires an investment in time and labor, and utilizing quality components from a rebuild kit that may cost a little more goes a long way toward having a successful result.

Novak Conversions is an excellent source for Dana 300 rebuild kits as well as others, and the company's complete rebuild kit was utilized to go through the process in this chapter. Advance Adapters, JB Conversions, and USA Standard Gear are also good sources for rebuild parts.

Disassembling a Dana 300 Transfer Case

1 ***After draining the fluid and removing the shifter assembly, start by pulling the front and rear output-shaft yokes, both of which are retained by a 1$^1/_8$-inch nut. Some manuals recommend using a gear puller to pull the yokes, but more often than not, lightly tapping the yokes outward from the backside with a mallet is sufficient to remove the yokes.***

Disassembling a Dana 300 Transfer Case *continued*

2 *Make careful note of the orientation of the speedometer-drive-gear housing. It's retained by a fork-shaped bracket and a single bolt, but the housing itself can be installed in one of three positions, depending on the diameter and tooth count of the drive gear inside. Make sure that it gets reinstalled in the same orientation during reassembly. If installed incorrectly, you run the risk of damaging the nylon drive gear and the speedometer not working. Remove the housing and set it aside, along with the retaining clip and bolt.*

3 *Flip over the case and remove the bottom inspection cover. On the back of the transfer case (roughly in the middle), you'll find a square block that engages the intermediate shaft retained by a small bolt. Remove the bolt and block. Then, use a brass drift and a mallet from the front of the case to drive the intermediate shaft rearward. The shaft must be removed and installed from the rear of the case. Do not attempt to drive the shaft forward because you will damage the case.*

4 *While driving the intermediate shaft rearward, you'll hear a bunch of needle bearings fall into the case. Don't panic because you'll be able to retrieve them later. Once the shaft has been removed, lift out the intermediate gear along with its thrust washers. There are one thick and two thin spacers mixed in with the needle bearings that fell into the case. A good rebuild kit includes new bearings, spacers, and an intermediate shaft.*

Disassembling a Dana 300 Transfer Case *continued*

5 *Next, pull the input-shaft gear and housing assembly. Most of the time, the input housing has two recesses machined in it that can be used to pry the housing out of the case after the bolts have been removed. Mine didn't have those recesses, and the input was really stuck in the housing. I ended up cutting two recesses in the housing to pry against, as it was the only way that the housing was going to come out.*

6 *Finish disassembling the input-gear assembly by removing the small snap ring from the input shaft, followed by the gear itself. Underneath the gear is a large snap ring that holds the input bearing in the aluminum housing. Remove the snap ring, and then the bearing can be lightly tapped out of the housing and off the shaft. This is important: there will likely be one or more shims present between the input shaft and bearing. Set these aside and save for reuse.*

Author: Please denote location where the arrow should be.

7 *Move to the rear output shaft. Remove the five 3/8-inch bolts that hold the rear output-shaft housing to the case and use a rubber mallet to break the seal between the housing and the case. Avoid the temptation to pry against the seal surface and potentially damage it. Make special note of the shims (arrow) that are against the outer bearing race and slide them off the shaft. These will be important later for initial endplay adjustment.*

8 Back in the main case, with the intermediate gear removed, you have access to the shift-fork set screws. Use an Allen socket with an extension to remove them. They will be tight and are held in place with thread-locking compound. Take care to not strip them out. Applying heat with a pencil torch may help loosen the screws, but be wary of flammables (such as gear oil) and an open flame.

9 Move to the front output bearing retainer. You have the option to twist the shift rails 90 degrees and gently pull them out. However, I prefer to pull the rails out after the retainer is removed from the case. Remove the bolts that secure the front retainer and gently break the seal with a rubber mallet. Again, be wary of prying against seal surfaces. Gently walk the front housing away from the case, being careful to ensure that the shift forks don't bind against the rails. They will, so use patience and a gentle touch. Don't force anything.

10 Remove the shift forks if you haven't already. Now, remove the rear bearing retainer for the front output shaft. It's secured with four bolts and there may be a number of shims behind the cap. Make careful note of the shims and set them aside for later because they are important for setting front output-shaft endplay. Remove the rear bearing race, which has a light slip-fit in the case.

Disassembling a Dana 300 Transfer Case *continued*

11 ***Slide the front output-shaft assembly toward the front of the case, with the face of the large gear flat against the inside of the case (as shown). Use a brass drift on the rear of the front output to drive the shaft forward, separating the rear bearing that is lightly press-fit on the shaft. The remaining front shaft assembly can now be removed from the case.***

12 ***The last bearing on the front output shaft can now be removed. Using a press and a bearing collar (as shown) is the easiest way to accomplish this. However, it can also be done with the creative placement of wood blocks and a dead-blow hammer or brass drift.***

13 ***The last piece of the puzzle is removing the rear output shaft. This can be done with a hydraulic press or with the case positioned on blocks of wood (as shown). Place the case on its face and ensure that the large gear on the output shaft is flush on the front of the case. Put a nut on the end of the shaft to help protect the threads. Then, use a dead-blow hammer, a brass drift, or an air hammer to drive the output shaft forward, pushing the remaining bearing off the shaft. I have had transfer cases that require a press for this step, as the bearing sometimes has a tight press fit. Once removed, the case is completely empty.***

14 *If you haven't done so already, remove the remaining bearing races and seals from the front and rear output bearing retainers as well as the front input housing. I used a brass drift to tap out the races. With this done, you can begin the long, laborious process of cleaning the case, the housings, and all of the internal gears.*

15 *If desired, you can remove the shift rails from the front housing to clean them and replace the seals as well as the shift poppet balls and springs. Remove the 4WD-indictor switch and its adjacent plug. Use a small screw-driver in the end of the shift rail to rotate each rail 90 degrees and pull them out of the housing. Be aware that the interlock pill may fight you if both rails aren't in neutral during the removal process. The spring-loaded poppet balls will likely fire directly at you during this process, so be careful and wear eye protection. My transfer case didn't jump out of gear or leak at the shift rails, so I left the rails alone.*

Inspecting a Dana 300 Transfer Case

1 *Inspect everything closely. Check for chipped or broken teeth on gears, evidence of bearings spinning on front or rear output shafts, and bent shift forks. Minor pitting on the gear faces usually isn't an issue, but major pitting is a cause for concern. Inspect the main case carefully, as they are known to crack. Look for cracks radiating from the inspection-cover hole as well as the intermediate-shaft bore and rear output bore. If you find any cracks, the case must be replaced. Replace any damaged gears, but note that sourcing individual gears may be difficult.*

2 *There is a roller bearing inside the bore of the output shaft. The roller bearing is difficult to remove but is also prone to wear and is an important component to replace during a major rebuild. A special tool, called a clutch pilot bearing puller, is needed to remove the bearing. However, there are alternative methods. One method is to pack the bore with grease or white bread (yes, actual bread) and then tap a rod that's close to the inside diameter of the bearing into the bore to hydraulically push the bearing out. You can also collapse the bearing with a narrow punch to eliminate its press fit, but be careful not to damage the bore with this method. I used a socket that is slightly smaller than the outside diameter of the bearing to tap the new one in place.*

Reassembling a Dana 300 Transfer Case

1 *After everything has been cleaned, reassembly can begin. Assemble the front output shaft and gear as shown and press on the new bearing. I used a short length of tubing to engage the inner race of the bearing so as not to damage it. You can also tap the bearing into place with tubing and a hammer, but a press ensures that the bearing is seated properly.*

2 *Lubricate all gear and bearing mating surfaces from this point forward during assembly. Place the front output shaft in the case and install the shift collar as well as the output shaft gear on the shaft. Note that the teeth for the clutch collar should face one another.*

3 *Position the case on wood blocks face down (as shown) and install the nut on the end of the output shaft to protect the threads. Verify that the input shaft cluster has been assembled properly (reference Step 2). Ideally, the end of the input shaft is resting on the bench and the assembly is "floating" in the case with no pressure on the case itself. Use a short length of pipe and a hammer to tap the rear bearing on to the front output shaft. A press can also be used for this step if desired.*

Reassembling a Dana 300 Transfer Case *continued*

4 *After installing a new roller bearing in the bore of the output shaft mentioned earlier, place the large output shaft gear in the case and then insert the rear output shaft through it. Slide the thrust washer onto the shaft (as shown), followed by the inner bearing. Don't forget that thrust washer!*

5 *Position the case face down on wood blocks and support the end of the input shaft (the end inside the case) on a smaller block of wood so that it's "floating" in the case with no pressure on the case itself. Use a piece of pipe to tap or press the inner bearing for the output shaft into place. It's important that this bearing is fully seated. Otherwise, it will be impossible to set endplay properly later.*

6 *Install a new seal into the input-shaft bearing retainer. Place the shim(s) that were present during removal on the input shaft. Tap or press the new bearing onto the input shaft, being careful to only apply pressure to the inner race of the bearing only to avoid damaging it. Now, tap or press the assembly into the aluminum input bearing retainer, this time applying pressure to the outer race of the bearing. Once seated, install the large snap ring into the groove of the retainer and be sure that it seats fully.*

7 *Lightly grease the splines on the input shaft. Orient the input shaft gear with the smaller outside-diameter portion of the gear facing up (as shown) and install the snap ring. Using a feeler gauge, check the gap between the rear face of the gear and the snap ring. There should be no more than 0.003 inch of clearance. If there is more than that, remove the gear and add shims between the input shaft and bearing until the desired clearance is achieved.*

8 *Install the remaining shift collar on the output-shaft assembly. Apply RTV sealant to the gasket surface of the input bearing retainer and attach the retainer to the main case using the original Allen-head bolts. Torque the bolts to 10 ft-lbs.*

9 *Note that when assembled properly, the front and rear output shaft cluster should look like this, with the shift collar gears facing one another and the shift collar in place.*

10 *Install the new bearing races in the rear tailhousing. Perform these next steps dry (no seals or sealant) until proper output-shaft endplay is achieved. Measure and make note of the thickness of the original shims that were on the rear output shaft (arrow). Start with that original thickness and assemble the rear tailhousing. Attach the tailhousing to the case using the original 3/8-inch bolts. Install the outer bearing in the foreground after the tailhousing is in place.*

11 *Install the output-shaft yoke and torque to 110 ft-lbs. Use a dial indicator to check output-shaft endplay. Place the pointer on the end of the shaft. Then, apply firm inward and outward (push/pull) pressure on the yoke to measure the amount of endplay. There should be no less than 0.002 inch and no more than 0.005 inch of endplay. If it's out of spec, remove the outer bearing and add or subtract shims until proper endplay is achieved. Adding shims increases endplay; subtracting shims reduces endplay. It may take several attempts, but achieving proper endplay is critical.*

12 *Once you've achieved proper endplay, remove the tailhousing and install the yoke seal as well as RTV sealant to the case's seal surface. Make sure that your final shims are in place and then attach the tailhousing for the final time (torque the bolts to 35 ft-lbs). Reinstall and torque the yoke. Then, check endplay one final time to be sure that it hasn't changed.*

13 *The shift forks have hard nylon wear pads to engage the shift collars, and quality rebuild kits include new pads. Once the new pads are in place, install the shift forks into the case. They should be positioned as shown, with the shorter of the two engaged with the front output shift collar and the larger positioned on the input/rear output shift collar. The larger fork will ultimately be positioned farther back in the case than the smaller fork.*

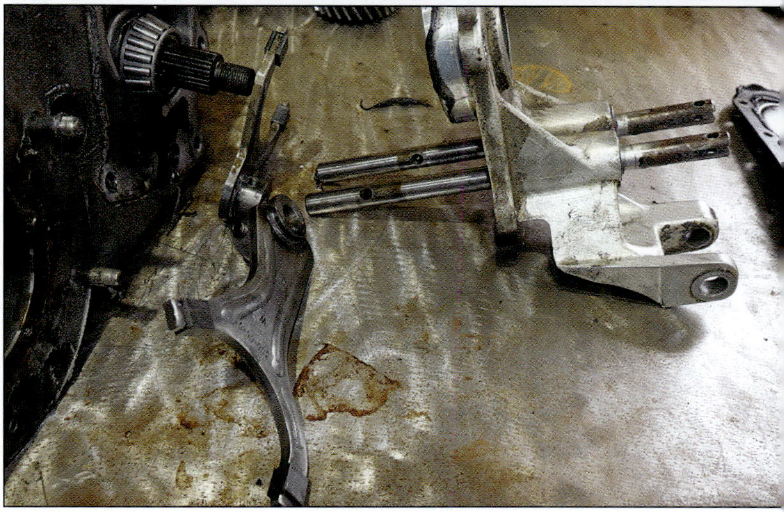

14 *If you choose, you can install the shift rails in the front output bearing retainer after it is in the case, but I found it easier to install them beforehand. Install new springs, poppet balls, and seals, making sure that the interlock pill is positioned properly. You ultimately want the rails positioned in neutral (rails centered and even with one another) as this disassembly photo shows. This is also another view of how the forks are oriented in the case.*

15 *Install the front bearing retainer gasket with RTV on both the case and the bearing retainer. Wrestling the front bearing retainer in place is tricky, and it's often helpful to have an extra set of hands. Guide the shift forks onto the rails while simultaneously trying to seat the front bearing retainer. The forks will likely bind up periodically, so be patient and don't use excessive force. Torque the bolts to 35 ft-lbs.*

16 *Front output-shaft endplay is controlled by shims positioned under the rear bearing cap. Begin with the original shim thickness (dry, no need for sealant yet) and secure the end cap using the original bolts (torque to 35 ft-lbs). Your rebuild kit should have included a variety of shims to make adjustments as necessary.*

17 *Checking front output-shaft endplay is similar to the rear, except that installing the yoke is not necessary. Tap the output shaft firmly inward and outward to measure end-play. As with the rear, proper spec is 0.002 inch to 0.005 inch. If adjustments are needed, remove the rear bearing cap and add or subtract shims as necessary. It make take several tries to achieve proper endplay, but this step is critical to the success of the rebuild.*

18 *Once you've obtained proper endplay, seal the rear cap. The design of the rear bearing cap leaves a lot to be desired and is a well-known source of leaks. The best chance for minimizing (note that I didn't say "eliminating") leakage is to apply a liberal coat of Permatex Copper Spray-A-Gasket to both sides or each shim as well as inside of the cap. Let the sealant tack up a bit before assembling and installing the shim stack for the final time.*

19 *Carefully line up the shift rails with the divots in the rails for the set screws. Apply thread-locking compound to the set screws. Then, install and tighten the screws firmly. Once in place, test the operation of the shift forks and visually verify that the collars move properly among the different shift positions.*

20 *Assemble the needle bearings and spacers in the bore of the intermediate gear. Use an engine assembly lube or frozen petroleum jelly for this step. Assemble 24 of the 48 bearings into the bore of the intermediate gear. Insert the thick spacer, and then assemble the other 24 rollers. There is a soft "snap" when you place the last bearing into position on each row. For clarification, the thick spacer will ultimately be between the two rows of roller bearings, and two thin spacers will be positioned on each outside edge. It also helps to grease the thrust washers (foreground) to help them stick to the sides of the case.*

Reassembling a Dana 300 Transfer Case *continued*

21 *Always use new roller bearings and a new intermediate shaft during a rebuild, as these are common wear points—even if they look okay visually. Also, never mix and match new and old bearings or shafts. One advantage of going with a quality rebuild kit, such as one from Novak, is an improved intermediate-shaft design. Note the O-ring grooves on both ends of the intermediate shaft versus a single groove on the stock one. This helps improve sealing.*

22 *It's beneficial to have an extra set of hands for this as well as a piece of bailing wire looped under the intermediate gear to help guide it up and down in the case. Position the greased thrust washers on the inside of the case and start the intermediate shaft in the back of the case (you can use it to help keep the rear thrust washer in place). Lower the intermediate gear into the case while trying to minimize displacing the thrust washers. It should be snug but go in by hand. Align the bore of the intermediate gear with the shaft and start tapping the shaft into place. Check to be sure all the rollers remain stacked as you continue tapping the shaft forward. Pay attention to the alignment of the slot on the end of the shaft and the position of the retaining block once the shaft is seated; it is difficult to rotate once more than about two-thirds of the way into the case.*

23 ***Once the intermediate gear is seated, install the retaining block and bolt for the intermediate shaft. Cycle the transfer case through all of its positions one final time, and be sure that the appropriate shafts rotate properly in the appropriate ranges. Position the inspection cover gasket and apply RTV or the Right Stuff to both sides of it before tightening the inspection cover.***

CHAPTER 5

NP231 Transfer Case Rebuild

The NP231 is substantially different from the other transfer cases that have been featured earlier in this book. First, it's a chain-driven transfer case, which means that the front output is driven by a chain rather than a series of gears that intermesh. Second, the entire exterior case is constructed of aluminum rather than cast iron. Third, it was manufactured by New Process Gear, which eventually changed its name to New Venture Gear following a merger and a reorganization.

Despite being used in Chevy, Dodge, and Jeep vehicles, all NP231s in stock form look just like this one: an aluminum case with an array of bolts that connect the two case halves. When searching for one in a junkyard, note that a number of other transfer cases look similar to the NP231, most of which are also manufactured by New Process (later New Venture) and have the same circular identification tag on the back. Always wipe off and look at the identification tag to make sure that you have an NP231 and not one of the many other cases that look similar but aren't the same.

As a result, working with the NP231 is different than working on the previous transfer cases, but it is also easier in many ways.

All of the bearings in this transfer case are caged rather than loose. Also, with just a few exceptions that are detailed in this chapter, all of the bearings are a loose slip-fit and are retained by snap rings rather than a pressed interference fit. Despite its modern design, the NP231 is one of the easiest transfer cases to rebuild. The only special tool that is needed is a good pair of snap-ring pliers. It's an ideal transfer case for a beginner who has never done transfer case work before.

Input Shaft

Pay attention to the input gear when swapping an NP231 transfer case. Jeep NP231s were either 21-spline in 4-cylinder applications or 23-spline in 6-cylinder applications. However, several different input-shaft lengths have been noted. I believe that the length differences come from the different transmissions that these cases were mated to, and there were quite a few both manual and automatics that were used through the years.

I have run across situations where the input shaft was too long or too short when attempting to swap an NP231 into a non-stock application. Plus, many

NP231 Gear Cut Variations

There is a variation in the way that the planetary and input gears are cut, depending on the year of the transfer case. This is not significant if you're simply going through a rebuild and aren't changing any internal gears, but if you're changing the input gear of an NP231 or upgrading to a six-pinion planetary, you should know. The difference is subtle but important because they are not interchangeable.

Transfer cases manufactured through 1993 have a slightly shallower cut in the planetary set that gives the tip of the teeth a blunt, flatter look. Starting in about 1994, New Process changed the depth of the gear cut, giving the tips of the teeth on planetaries and input gears a sharper, pointier tip. The difference is subtle and can be difficult to detect without seeing the two variations side by side. Again, the difference is critically important.

It's possible to install a mismatched planetary set in the ring gear pressed into the case, and it's somewhat possible to install a mismatched input gear into a planetary set, but rotating the gears will feel rough and very notchy.

Despite what is written on the internet or seen on YouTube, these two gear variations are not interchangeable. Using mismatched gears leads to a noisy transfer case and premature failure. If you want to upgrade to a six-pinion planetary, and especially if you need to change the input gear of your transfer case, use components with the gear cut that matches your transfer case.

So, how do you determine the build date of the transfer case? If you know the year of the vehicle that the transfer case came from, it's safe to assume that the transfer case is the same year. Otherwise, you may be able to decode the part number or assembly number on the round silver tag on the back of the case. However, the 1993/1994 split is not an absolute; instead, it's a guideline. If you're working with a transfer case that is near this year split or you are just unsure, disassemble the case and inspect the gears. ■

Look closely at the way the teeth of these two planetaries are shaped. The gear teeth on the left have relatively blunt, flat tips, while the teeth on the right planetary have more of a sharper, narrower tip. The blunt, flatter teeth are indicative of transfer cases that were manufactured up to (and including) 1993. The more pointy teeth indicate an NP231 that was manufactured starting in 1994 and continuing to the end of the NP231's production run. This year break is not absolute. Instead, it's a general guideline to use when searching for upgrades, replacement parts, or when swapping input gears. These two gear variations are not interchangeable.

aftermarket adapters can require an input of a certain length. Check the spline engagement if you're working with a non-stock application. In some cases, inputs that are too long can simply be cut down, but in other cases, you may need to swap the input gear, which requires complete transfer case disassembly. Note that all NP231 input gears and most NP241 input gears are interchangeable, but be sure to check out the "NP231 Gear Cut Variations" sidebar in this chapter regarding the year split variation for gear cuts.

Note that I obtained the basic rebuild for this kit from Advance Adapters as well as the SYE kit. The chain upgrade that is detailed was obtained from an online marketplace.

Opening the Case

When working with an NP231, keep the following things in mind. First, they seal up well, much better than most of the previous transfer cases that Jeep used. There are no gaskets used with an NP231, as the entire case relies upon using silicone at the sealing surfaces. As a result, the case halves and the rear output housing are often "stuck" together and can be difficult to separate.

The best method of breaking these seals is to 1) make sure that all of the bolts are removed and 2) find a prying point between the two components to pop the seal. Once the seal is broken, the components generally come apart easily. There are usually strategic prying points built into the case design to help facilitate this, so take some time to find them. At all costs, avoid the urge to wedge a screwdriver or a pry bar directly into a sealed joint! Remember that these cases are aluminum, and the seal surfaces can be damaged easily, causing leaks.

Cleaning the Case

Since these cases rely on only RTV sealant, cleaning the sealing surfaces is critically important. The best cleaning method is using a razor-blade scraper and a lot of patience. Do not use abrasive discs of any kind, including Scotch-Brite pads! Aluminum is soft, and it's very easy to remove material from the gasket surfaces and warp them to the point that they are no longer flat. I have seen rubberized discs designed for cleaning aluminum head surfaces used with success. These have little rubberized fingers, or nubs, that can remove sealant without damaging the aluminum. However, they are difficult to find.

NP241

Although this rebuild procedure covers an NP231, the process is nearly identical to the NP241, which is basically a beefed-up version of the NP231 that was used in many Chevy and Dodge trucks. There are also striking similarities in design and construction among nearly all of the chain-driven transfer cases made by New Process, of which there are many. After going through an NP231, a competent shade-tree mechanic should have no problem going through an NP208, NP242, and several others.

Disassembling an NP231 Transfer Case

1 *Begin the disassembly by removing the three bolts that hold the slip housing on the rear output shaft. It may take a few light taps with a rubber mallet to break the silicone seal after the bolts have been removed. With the tailhousing removed, you will see the first of many snap rings that you'll encounter during this rebuild. In this case, it's the snap ring that retains the rear output bearing to the tailshaft. Remove that snap ring. Investing in a good large pair of snap-ring pliers is essential for working with these transfer cases.*

2 *Remove the speedometer drive gear from the tailhousing. Then, remove the five bolts that hold the tailhousing to the back of the case. There are wings present on the tailhousing that you can pry against to break the silicone seal. The tailhousing with the bearing still in it will slide off the output shaft. Set these parts aside for the moment and save all hardware for reuse.*

Disassembling an NP231 Transfer Case *continued*

3 *With the tailhousing removed, you can see the oil pump, which is a thin disc-shaped piece with a splined center. Gently remove the pickup tube from the pump and slide the pump off the shaft (or you can leave it in place until you separate the back half of the case). This pump is not a serviceable item, so do not take it apart. It's also easily damaged, so be careful with it.*

4 *Remove the eight bolts that secure the rear case half to the front case half (the perimeter bolts around the outside of the case). As with the tailhousing, the case halves are sealed with silicone. Avoid sticking a screwdriver between the case halves to break the seal because that will damage the gasket surface and cause leaks. A pry point was cast into the case near the front output shaft (pictured) that you can use to break the seal. Once broken, you can lift off the rear case half without drama.*

5 *With the rear case half removed, you can see the chain, front and rear outputs, and the shift fork. If you haven't done so already, remove the nut for the front output-shaft yoke along with the yoke. Make careful note of the arrangement of everything and maybe even snap a few photos for reference. Give the front shaft a few taps with a rubber mallet to unseat it from the front bearing. Then, with the help of an assistant, grab the front and rear output shafts and lift the entire assembly out of the case. The front and rear outputs, chain, and shift fork come out as an assembly.*

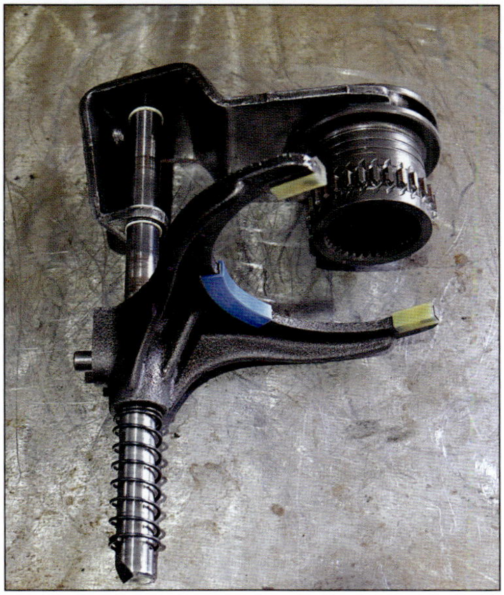

6 *For reference, this is the arrangement of the shift fork as it will come out of the case. The lower portion of the shift-fork assembly and gear may stay in the case when you remove the mainshaft. Just know it should be positioned in the same manner during reassembly.*

7 *This is another view of the lower portion of the shift assembly, which may or may not remain in the case when you remove the mainshaft. Note that the pin in the fork engages a slot in the sector shaft attached to the shift lever on the outside of the case. The sector shaft and shift assembly normally do not require any service, unless there's a shifting issue.*

Disassembling an NP231 Transfer Case *continued*

8 *This is the mainshaft assembly as it should have been removed from the case. Make note that the thick end of the shift collar (the part with the groove where the shift fork rides) faces toward the front of the case and away from the end of the output shaft (where the yoke would be positioned).*

9 *Remove the shift collar from the mainshaft assembly. It should be removable by hand. Underneath the shift collar are spring-loaded shift dogs, and depending on the year of the case, a brass shift collar may be visible. Later versions often don't have the brass collar.*

10 *If the springs and shift dogs look good and you are not doing an SYE kit, reinstall the shift collar, set the assembly aside, and skip ahead several steps. If you are using an SYE kit, remove the snap ring that holds the large outer gear to the mainshaft. This one often takes time, patience, and a good pair of snap-ring pliers to remove. Once dislodged, the snap ring and outer gear can be removed, followed by the brass shift collar (if present).*

Measuring Chain Stretch

As with any other moving part, the chain inside of an NP231 transfer case is a wear item. It's constantly spinning even in 2WD, so mileage is a factor for chain wear even in a vehicle where 4WD is rarely used.

With that being said, you don't often hear about NP231s with a worn-out chain, except in applications where 4WD is used extensively, such as in cold climates or applications used to plow snow for many years. A worn-out chain can be detected if you see witness or wear marks on the inside of the case where the chain has been rubbing on it, a grinding or humming sound at freeway speeds, or a loud popping noise (in extreme cases) when the case is placed under a heavy load in 4WD.

There are probably more scientific means for measuring chain wear, but this method works well. Hold the chain by one end on its side and observe the amount of droop at the other. The chain should remain pretty straight and not droop more than a degree or two. If it droops more than that, replace the chain.

The chain can be checked for excessive stretch in two ways. One is to hold the front and rear output shafts and then try to rotate the front output. If you can rotate the front output more than about a quarter of a turn, the chain is shot. The second method works with the chain removed. Hold the chain sideways on one end. If the chain droops more than a degree or two from staying perfectly flat, replace the chain.

New chains are available but are not normally part of a rebuild kit. If you must replace the chain, consider upgrading to a 1¼-inch chain for extra strength. ■

Inspecting an NP231 Transfer Case

1 ***A stock mainshaft (top) and an SYE mainshaft (bottom) are shown for comparison. The most obvious difference is that the stock mainshaft is much longer than the new one. Once installed, the SYE kit will add 3½ to 4 inches in driveline length, which is a real benefit in lifted short-wheelbase applications. This also allows the use of a CV joint at the transfer case, which can handle more driveline angle than a conventional driveshaft with regular U-joints at both ends.***

2 *This closer view reveals further improvements. Note how the stock mainshaft necks down significantly where the spiral-cut gears for the speedometer are located. This is a significant weak point and is a common source of failure. Note how the SYE shaft is much thicker with straight-cut gears in this same area. This is a major strength improvement that is not addressed with less expensive "hack-and-tap" SYE kits that cut down the stock mainshaft. This is why true SYE kits with a replacement mainshaft are much better.*

3 *Comparing the new tailhousing further reinforces just how much overall transfer case length is reduced (and driveline length is increased) with an SYE kit. The SYE tailhousing on the left is significantly shorter. The longer driveline, the strength improvement, and the ability to retain transfer-case fluid in the event of a driveline failure make an SYE kit a no-brainer decision to use on anything other than a stock application.*

4 *Another worthwhile upgrade to consider is installing a wider chain to drive the front output shaft. Stock NP231s, like those in most Jeeps, came with a 1-inch-wide chain (top), while HD versions of the NP231 usually came with a 1¼-inch-wide chain (bottom). Strength estimates vary, but it's safe to assume that the wider chain is good for about a 20-percent strength improvement over the stock chain. While not necessary for a mild build, if your build includes V-8 power, big tires, and low gearing, upgrading to the wider chain is worthwhile.*

5 *These are the components that are required to accomplish the wider chain upgrade along with the stock components next to them. You'll need a new front output shaft (bottom left), chain (bottom), and new drive sprocket for the mainshaft (middle left). These upgrade parts can be sourced from a variety of places. I obtained these from a seller on eBay.*

6 *Early versions of the NP231 (mostly in YJs and early 1990s XJs) have caged needle bearings pressed into the chain drive sprocket, while later NP231s, such as those in TJs and later XJs, did not. Most rebuild kits include these bearings and they can easily be pressed in and out of their bores. Most SYE kits, including mine, are based on the later TJ style, so these bearings must be removed but are not replaced.*

7 *Inspect the shift dogs and retaining springs in the mode hub. The springs are relatively lightweight and may have become dislodged during removal. The springs themselves are lightweight but should engage each shift dog. There are two springs, one on each side of the hub.*

Inspecting an NP231 Transfer Case *continued*

8 ***As stated earlier, most SYE kits are built around the later TJ-style NP231 that does not use needle bearings on the drive sprocket, so remove them if you haven't already. Lubricate the mainshaft lightly and slide the drive sprocket on the mainshaft in the orientation shown.***

Reassembling an NP231 Transfer Case

1 ***If there is a brass shift collar present and you aren't upgrading to a wider chain, slide the shift collar into place followed by the mode hub assembly. These should slide easily into place and reveal the recess for the snap ring to hold them in place. A quality rebuild kit will include new snap rings, which you should be using. Make sure the ring is fully seated in its groove. Mainshaft assembly is now complete. Set it aside for now.***

2 ***Regarding the brass synchro ring, some NP231s have them and some don't, so don't be alarmed if yours doesn't. My 1¼-inch chain drive sprocket came with a note that it's not compatible with the ring and advised removing it, so I did. If yours had one stock and you're not upgrading, reinstall it. There is little to no difference in shifting performance with or without the ring that I've noted.***

Reassembling an NP231 Transfer Case *continued*

3 *Flip the front case half over with the input gear facing up. Remove the four bolts retaining the seal housing to the case and then use the recess to gently pry up on the housing to break the silicone seal. The seal housing can then be removed and cleaned up, and a fresh seal can be installed.*

4 *With the input seal housing removed, you can access the inner snap ring that retains the input gear to the input bearing and the outer snap ring that retains the bearing to the housing. Removing the inner snap ring allows the input gear and planetary assembly to be removed from the case. Removing the outer snap ring allows the bearing to be tapped out of the case.*

5 *The input gear is retained in the planetary assembly via, you guessed it, another snap ring. Removing the snap ring allows the input gear to be removed from the planetary set. If you're replacing the input gear, now is the time to do so. Make careful note of the position of the plastic thrust washers and replace them with new ones supplied with your rebuild kit. Then, reinstall the snap ring. There is a bearing inside the input gear that is very difficult to remove and usually doesn't need to be replaced unless the vehicle has been used for extremely long periods in low range.*

Reassembling an NP231 Transfer Case *continued*

6 *The 2.72 low range in the NP231 is accomplished via a compact and strong planetary gearset. A standard NP231 is equipped with three planetary gears. However, the HD and even some standard versions were equipped with a significantly stronger six-pinion planetary. Upgrading to a six-pinion planetary is a drop-in affair as long as you're mindful of the early/late-year split (see the "NP231 Gear Cut Variations" sidebar). Note that the outside ring gear (the part the planetary set slides into) is pressed into the transfer case housing and is not removable without highly specialized tools. If it's damaged, find a different case.*

7 *Install a new bearing in the case for the front input and secure it with a new snap ring. Once done, the input/planetary assembly can be reinstalled in the case, with the input shaft easily sliding through the inside diameter of the input gear. It should look just like this, and once it has been seated, the assembly can be secured with a snap ring on the input shaft, seating the shaft to the input bearing. If you've swapped the input or planetary gearset, rotate the assembly. It should rotate smoothly and not feel rough or notchy.*

8 *Clean the surfaces of the front input seal housing and its mating surface on the case. Apply RTV silicone (I like Permatex's The Right Stuff) to the seal housing and resecure it using the four original bolts.*

9 ***Remove and replace the front input shaft bearing (if you have not done so already). The front output-shaft seal (pictured) is very difficult to remove but is a common source of leaks and should always be replaced. I ended up having to collapse the seal with a punch, being careful not to mar the easily damaged outer seal surface in the housing.***

10 ***Once the seal has been removed, you can access the snap ring that holds the front output shaft bearing in the case. Remove the snap ring, tap out the old bearing, install the new one, and reinstall the snap ring. Use a piece of tubing or a large socket to install the new outer seal.***

Reassembling an NP231 Transfer Case *continued*

11 *Position the front case half on the bench face down. Reference Step 7 of the disassembly photos to position the lower shift mechanism in the case and be sure that the pin in the mechanism is engaged in the shift actuator. Install new wear pads on the shift fork if they are provided in your rebuild kit. You can test fit the fork assembly in the case as shown, but it will need to be installed with the mainshaft assembly in the next step.*

12 *An extra set of hands is helpful for this step. Gather and position the mainshaft assembly, shift fork, chain, and front output shaft as one unit and slide the entire assembly into the case. This all has to be installed together because there won't be enough slack in the chain to install the mainshaft first and then the front output later. As you lower everything into the case, be sure that the shift fork seats in the lower fork assembly. It takes some patience, but everything drops right into place if it's positioned correctly.*

13 *By far the most difficult bearing to replace in an NP231 is the rear bearing for the front output shaft, which is pressed into the rear case half. It has a very tight press fit, and the only correct way to remove it is with a blind bearing puller. I purchased a decent puller on the internet, but it still required heating the case with MAPP gas to get the bearing out.*

14 *This is another view of the puller with the bearing removed. It's an expanding collet that grabs the backside of the bearing and then is attached to a slide hammer. This is the only non-destructive way I've found to remove this bearing, although I have heard of people carefully cutting it with a Dremel tool. Most other removal methods will inevitably damage the case.*

Reassembling an NP231 Transfer Case *continued*

15 *I strongly recommend putting the new rear input bearing in a freezer for several hours to ease installation. Use the old bearing or a socket of the appropriate outside diameter to then install the new bearing in the rear case half. Note that the bearing is slightly recessed in the case when fully seated.*

16 *Thoroughly clean the gasket mating surfaces of the front and rear case halves if you haven't already. As noted earlier, do not use abrasive wheels on soft aluminum. Clean the oil-pump screen of any debris or residue and position it in the rear case half (as shown). Don't forget to clean and reinstall the circular magnet in its recess in the front case half as well.*

17 *If you're working with an older transfer case (such as from a YJ or XJ), test fit the rear case half and shift the transfer case so that the shift fork sticks out from the back of the case as far as it will go. Measure the amount of shift fork that protrudes from the case. Most SYE kits accommodate no more than 1 inch of stick-out length. If the amount of length that sticks out past the case is greater than 1 inch (as it was here), the fork must be shortened to 1 inch using a hacksaw or cutoff wheel. I used a piece of tape as a cutting guide.*

18 *Apply a bead of silicone sealant to the entire perimeter of the front case half. Avoid using an excessive amount because the silicone can end up plugging the oil pump. Position the oil pump on the rear case half and seat the oil pump pickup tube into the pump O-ring. Line up the rear case half with the front as well as the oil pump on the mainshaft and secure the two halves together using the original hardware. Do not force anything during this process! Once seated, torque the bolts to 20 to 25 ft-lbs in roughly a star pattern.*

19 *In the case of an SYE kit, once the rear case half and oil pump are secure, install the speedometer drive gear. The gear can be installed in either direction and is secured to the mainshaft with a snap ring.*

20 *If you have not done so already, install the rear output-shaft bearing, retaining snap ring, and output-shaft yoke seal on the tailhousing. Apply a thin bead of silicone sealant to the face of the tailhousing (again, avoid the urge to use an excessive amount) and secure the tailhousing to the rear case half. Pay close attention, as the oil pump has outer tabs on it that must line up with recesses in the tailhousing for everything to seat properly. Torque the bolts to 15 to 20 ft-lbs.*

21 *Install a rubber star washer on the end of the rear output shaft and lightly grease the outer yoke surface before sliding the yoke into place and securing it with a new nut. Torque to 140 to 150 ft-lbs. Do the same thing for the front output yoke. Lastly, check your work by shifting the transfer case into each gear and checking for proper operation. Note that the shift lever will feel stiff but should engage each gear firmly. Rotating the front or rear output may be necessary to assist with shifting between modes.*

Source Guide

Advance Adapters
advanceadapters.com
800-350-2223

Herm the Overdrive Guy
hermtheoverdriveguy.com
360-256-3843

JB Conversions
Jbconversions.com
337-625-2379

Mile Marker
milemarker.com
800-886-8647

Novak Conversions
novak-adapt.com
877-602-1500

Teraflex
teraflex.com
801-713-3314

Tom Woods Driveshafts
4xshaft.com
801-737-0757

USA Standard Gear
usastandardgear.com
888-804-5774